OSHO

A CUP OF TEA

Letters written by Osho to disciples and friends

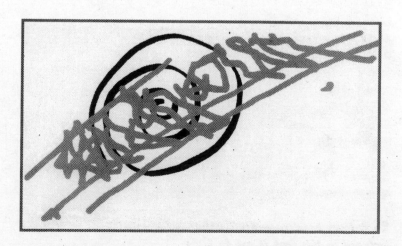

Editing: Ma Prem Maneesha and Ma Yoga Sudha
Design & Coordination: Swami Amano Surdham
Hindi letters translated by: Swami Anand Maitreya and
Swami Yoga Pratap Bharati

Phototypesetting by
Tao Publishing Pvt. Ltd.,
50 Koregaon Park, Pune-1
ISBN 81-7182-731-4
Published by
Diamond Pocket Books Pvt. Ltd.
X-30, Okhla Industrial Area,
Phase II, New Delhi-20

Printed by
Adarsha Printers, Naveen Shahdara, Delhi-32

Price: Rs. **150/-**

*Back cover painting and all paintings/signatures
included in this book is art by Osho*

A monk came to the Zen Master Joshu who asked:
Have you ever been here ?
The monk said: No, master.

Joshu said to him:
HAVE A CUP OF TEA,
O MY BROTHER.

Another monk called
and the Master again said;
Have you ever been here?
Yes, Master, was the answer.

The Master said:
HAVE A CUP OF TEA,
O MY BROTHER.

INTRODUCTION

The first time I gave a cup of tea to Osho I was so nervous, that I made the tea too fast, poured it too soon and presented it stone-cold. He accepted it graciously, drank it as though it was the most delicious tea He had ever had, and made a remark so subtle about its temperature, that it wasn't until I was outside His room, spinning down the corridor to the kitchen in a haze of bliss and fresh minty fragrance, that I realized the tea had been cold, but He drank it! He could have said, "Ugh! bring me a fresh cup," but He accepted my cold cup of tea with such grace and love, and yet got the message across to me not to do it that way again; without even hurting my feelings.

This 'Cup of Tea' is filled with awareness and love — the love and compassion of the enlightened master for anyone who is thirsty for a spiritual life. Osho encourages us to move more into meditation, as He shares the insights and experiences that He has had on the path.

In this book are 365 letters that Osho wrote to disciples, friends and lovers while He was travelling in India from 1951 through the 1970's.

Even while He was working as a professor at university He would travel to different towns giving as many as five lectures a day; sometimes to crowds as large as 50,000 and sometimes just to small groups. At times the people would be antagonistic, and sometimes they would worship Him, and that could mean not leaving Him alone for even two minutes — massaging His feet,

Bhagwan Shree Rajneesh is now known simply as Osho.

Osho has explained that His name is derived from William James' word 'oceanic' which means dissolving into the ocean. Oceanic describes the experience, He says, but what about the experiencer? For that we use the word 'Osho'. Later He came to find out that 'Osho' has also been used historically in the Far East meaning "The Blessed One, on whom the Sky Showers Flowers."

asking questions, wanting to be with Him. During these years Osho was also starting meditation centres and leading meditation camps.

And yet...he found time to write hundreds of letters to disciples and friends He met along the way, urging them to continue on the path: "I was once there too...I have travelled those same paths...Many times one be-comes disheartened on the path...."

He answers questions like, "What is mind? How to become free of thoughts?"

What has happened to Him – could it happen to us? Osho insists that it can. Nowhere and never do you find Him setting Himself up as essentially something special, extraordinary, a messiah. Instead He coaxes, persuades, provokes, spurs, encourages, leads and inspires – even charms and seduces us into finding the divine within ourselves.

Without any intellectual jargon, without any philosophical explanation or any psychological breakdown of the meaning of love; the understanding of that rare relationship between the master and disciple is there on every page, shining through, the way invisible ink reveals it's secrets before the heat of a flame.

Each letter is to be savored, sipped, and with closed eyes, pondered upon – for each letter contains a great teaching, a key to inner mysteries.

As I read, the words "I am in complete bliss" keep leaping off the pages at me. And Osho must have been, for how else could He possibly have so much love for everyone, how else could He have the energy to travel all over India – every village from North to South, East to West, "Looking for my people," He says.

I have a perpetual smile on my face while reading this book and I am in wonder at the astounding capacity Osho has for putting bliss into words. He is in love. He is in love with everyone and everything. And it is contagious.

Names of all respondents, save a few, have been omitted, as have named references in the letters themselves, on the grounds that Osho is addressing us all, all of the time. Each letter is to you and to me, not to him and her – as you will discover.

Also, certain Sanskirt/Hindi words have been retained, such as: *sadhana, rishi, samadhi, moksha, nirvana, samsara, leela, sannyas.* These words cannot be properly translated, and in any case are finding their way into the English language as Westerners in large numbers tune into the eternal truths found so vividly and in such abundance in writings of the East.

"When there is love, space and time vanish…" Osho says in one of these letters. And, yes, this is what I feel when reading this book – that I enter a timeless dimension.

Ma Prem Shunyo

1962

1.

Love.
I received your letter.
How lovingly you insist on my writing something,
and here am I, drowned in a deep silence!
I speak, I work,
but I am steeped in emptiness within.
There, there is no movement.
Thus I seem to be living two lives at one time.
What a drama!
But perhaps all of life is a drama
and becoming aware of this opens the door
to a unique freedom.

That which is
inaction in action
stillness in motion
eternity in change
— that is truth
and that *is existence*.
Real life lies in this eternity —
everything else is just the stream of dreams.
In truth the world is just a dream
and the question is not whether to leave
these dreams or not,
one just has to be aware of them.

With this awareness, everything changes.
The center moves.
A shift takes place from body to soul.
And what is *there?*
It cannot be told.
It has never been told
and it never will be.

There is no other way but to know it for oneself.
Death is known only through dying
and truth is known only through diving
deep within oneself.
May God drown you in this truth!

2.

Love.
I am in bliss.
I have been meaning to write for a long time
but many engagements prevented me.
My blessings, however, I send every day.

Life is a *sadhana;*
the more you involve yourself in it
the more divine it becomes.
The light is hidden in the darkness,
truth is hidden,
and from this comes the joy of searching.

I remember the words of a *rishi:*
Truth is hidden under a golden lid.
The golden lid that hides truth is nothing but our mind.
The mind has smothered us;
we are in it,
we identify with it,
therefore the suffering comes,
the bondage and the chain of rebirths.

Rise above it,
become aware that you are distinct from it –
that alone brings bliss,
that alone is freedom
and the end of birth and death.

We have to be what we truly are:

this is the only *sadhana*.
It is the frustration of living through desires
that brings this *sadhana*.

Become alert about desire
and non-attachment begins to appear.
This is not to be made to happen,
it follows naturally from awareness of attachment.
Each one of us has to become aware of his attachments,
and keep being so!
Nothing should be done unconsciously.

If this is remembered
one day a totally new kind of revolution takes place
in our consciousness.
God is leading you towards this revolution —
this I know.

3.

My respects to you.
I was extremely pleased to get your letter.
So far I have not written anything
but a meditation center has started here
where some friends are experimenting.
When I have some definite results
there is every possibility of my writing something.

About my experiments on myself, I am sure and certain,
but I want to test their usefulness to others.
I do not want to write anything
in the manner of philosophy,
my outlook is scientific.
I want to say something about yoga
based on certain psychological
and parapsychological experiments.
There are many illusory notions held about it

and these have to be refuted.
Therefore I am experimenting here also.

It is clear to me
that this work is not for promoting any group or cause.

If you ever come here we can talk more about all this.

4.

My respects to you.
I am grateful for your affectionate letter.
You are meditating – that is a matter for joy.
Drop all ideas of *achieving* in meditation,
just do it naturally;
what happens, happens on its own.
One day, effortlessly,
everything starts happening by itself.
Effort does not lead to meditation,
in fact it is a hindrance.
In effort, practice, study,
there is tension.
Any expectation,
even the expectation of peace,
brings restlessness.
The tension has to go.
As soon as this happens
a divine peace sets in.

Stop feeling: *I am doing it;*
realize instead: *I leave myself in the hands of that-which-is.*
Surrender,
surrender yourself completely;
as soon as you do this, emptiness comes.

Breathing and the body are becoming relaxed, you say.
This will happen with the mind too.

When the mind goes
what takes place is indescribable.

I know that this is going to happen to you both.
Just go on naturally and without purpose.
Soon I shall be there,
until then, go on quietly with what I have told you to do.

My respects to all.
Write whenever you feel like it.
I am in complete bliss.

5.

Love.
It is through God's grace
that you are working towards the discovery
of the inner light.
That light is definitely there
and once it is met all darkness in life disappears.
Each step taken within
peels away the darkness layer by layer
unfolding a world of light in which everything is new.
This experience cuts away all bondage –
and then comes the realization that it was never there!
Liberation happens to that which is eternally free!

I am pleased with your progress.
Your letter was received long back
but as I was busy there was delay in replying,
but my memory of you is always there,
along with all those eager for the light.
My good wishes flow for ever towards them.

We have to keep going.
Many times
one becomes disheartened on the path

but ultimately
the thirsty pilgrim reaches the spring.
In fact the water is there before the thirst.

My kind regards to all.

6.

My respects to you.
I was away, but your letter followed me here.
I am pleased to have it.

I see life as full of bliss.
Ordinarily, we do not have the eyes to see this
and so are deprived of it,
but this *seeing* can be created.
Perhaps it is not correct to say it can be *created*;
it is already there,
it is only a matter of opening the eyes,
and then – everything changes.

Meditation achieves this.

Meditation means: peace; emptiness.
This emptiness is there
but is concealed by the flow of thoughts.
As thoughts cease it comes into view.
It seems difficult to become free of thoughts
but it is very simple.
The mind seems very restless
but it can easily settle.
The key to this transcendence is *witnessing*.
One has to be a witness,
an observer of the mind.

One has to watch it,
just watch it.

The moment the witness state dawns,
that very moment one becomes free of thoughts.
This in turn opens the door to bliss
and then this very world changes
into a new world altogether.

Keep meditating.
Results will come slowly.
You are not to worry about that,
their coming is certain.

My kind regards to all.

7.

Love.
It is a long time since I received your letter.
I am happy that you long for peace –
but drop this idea that you are way behind.
Nobody is lagging behind.

It is just a matter of turning in –
and the drop becomes the ocean.
Actually the drop is the ocean
but it does not know it –
that is the only separation.
In the emptiness of meditation even this separation goes.
Meditation is the center of life's *sadhana*.

The thought process will slow down
and in its place will come peace and emptiness.
When thoughts vanish
the seer, the witness, becomes visible
and the complex of the unconscious disappears.
This complex is the cause of bondage.
In the beginning it appears as hard as stone
but the seeker who practices patiently

finds one day that it was just a dream, a puff of air.
May the seed of your meditation
blossom into the flower of *samadhi!*
My kind regards to all.
The rest when we meet.

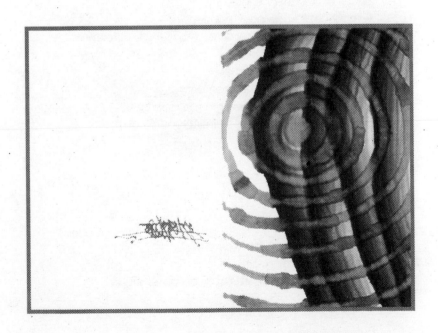

1963

8.

My respects to you.
Moving around for the whole of May affected my health so all
programs for June – Bombay, Calcutta, Jaipur – were cancelled.

I am glad to hear you are experimenting with
samadhi yoga.
Don't worry about results,
just be with the experimenting.
The return is bound to come one day – not gradually
but all of a sudden, effortlessly,
without one's knowing, it happens.
Within a moment life becomes wonderfully different!

I am not writing anything on
Bhagwan Mahavir at the moment.
There is no urge whatsoever in me to write.
But if you persuade me it is a different thing!
Everything else is fine.

9.

Love
I read your letter on the way here.
It has touched my heart.
If your desire to know life's truth becomes strong
then what is longing today
becomes one day the attainment.
Burning desire is all that is needed
and nothing else.
As rivers seek out the ocean
so man if he wants to can find the truth.
No peak, no mountain can stop him,

in fact their challenge awakens his sense of adventure.
Truth is within everyone.
Rivers have to find the ocean
but our ocean is inside us –
it is a wonder that so many remain thirsty still without it.
Actually they cannot really want it.
There is a saying of Christ's: Ask and ye shall receive.
But if you don't ask, whose fault is it?
There is no better bargain than the attainment of God.
We have only to ask, nothing more.
As the asking grows stronger and stronger
so he who asks starts vanishing.
A limit is reached,
a point of evaporation is reached,
where the seeker utterly disappears
and only the asking remains.
This is the very moment of attainment.

Truth is where the I is not –
this experience alone is the divine experience.
Absence of ego is presence of God.

My regards to all there.

10.

My respects to you.
I was waiting for your letter when it came.
I really want your life to be filled with light,
for you to surrender yourself to God.
God and light are always close by.
It is only a matter of opening one's eyes
and then what is ours becomes ours.
The distance is just that of
between the eyelash and the eye –
and perhaps not even that much;
the eyes are always open, only we don't know it.

There is an old story:
A fish had long heard stories about the ocean.
She began to fret about it
so one day she asked the Queen of Fishes:
What is this ocean and where is it?
The Queen was surprised. She said:
The ocean? Why, you are in the ocean itself!
Your very existence, your very life, is in the ocean.
It is within you.
The ocean is your everything,
but for the ocean, you are nothing.

For this very reason
the fish couldn't see the ocean!
And for this very reason
we are unable to find God.

But he can be found –
by being empty.
In the state of emptiness we meet him
for God is emptiness.

I am in bliss,
or shall I say –
Bliss alone is and I am not!

11.

My respects to you.
I received your letter, I was waiting for it.
The trip to Rajnagar was blissful.

Religion robbed of the spirit of yoga
has become a matter of morality only,
thereby losing its soul.
Morality is negative.

Life cánnot be based on negation,
negation cannot nourish life.

The emphasis has to be on attainment
not on renunciation.
It is not a question of renouncing ignorance
but of attaining understanding,
it is this that has to be central.
Practice has to be positive
and this *sadhana* can happen through yoga.

In my talks with Acharya Tulsi,
Muni Shri Nathamaljee and others
I have stressed this point.
Many letters have come from Rajnagar and Rajasthan
in this connection; as you have said
it seems some fruitful work has been accomplished
by going there.
One thing is very clear:
people are eager for a spiritual life
and current forms of religion do not satisfy them.
If however the right religion is given to them
it can revolutionize human consciousness.

I think of you.
May God grant you peace.
My love and regards to all.

12.

My respects to you.
All your letters arrived in good time
but as I have been busy I could not reply sooner.
I have been out most of the time
and I have just returned after speaking in Jaipur, Burhanpur,
Hoshangabad, Chanda
and other places.

How thirsty people are for spiritual life!
Seeing this
I am surprised that some people say
man has lost all interest in religion.
This can never be.
No interest in religion means no interest in life,
bliss, the ultimate.
Consciousness is by nature God-oriented
and it can only be satisfied by attaining God —
the state of *satchitananda*,
the truth-awareness-bliss state of being.

Hidden within one in the form of a seed
is the very source of religious birth,
therefore whilst religions may come and go
religion can never die.

I am glad to know that you feel patient
about your progress towards the light.
Patience is the most important thing of all
in spiritual life.
How long one must wait after sowing the seed!
At first all the effort seems wasted,
nothing seems to happen, and then one day
the waiting ends and there is actuality —
the seed breaks, pushes through the earth, into a plant!
But remember that even when nothing seemed to be happening the seed was working away under the soil.

It is the same with the seeker for truth —
when nothing appears to be happening
much is happening.
The fact is that all growth of life-energy
is unseen and unknown.
Only the results can be observed not the progress.

I am in bliss.
I want you to come closer to God.

Forget about results, just keep going on your path;
let the fruits come by themselves.
One day one wonders: What has happened!
What was I!
What have I become!
Compared to the results all the effort seems negligible.

My love to all.

13.

My respects to you.
I have just returned from Rajnagar in Rajasthan.
I was invited to a religious function there
organized by Acharya Shree Tulsi.
I put four hundred monks and nuns
through an experiment in meditation.
The results were extraordinary.

In my view, meditation is the essence
of all religious practice.
All the rest –
such as non-violence, renunciation of wealth, celibacy etc. –
are just its consequences.
With the attainment of *samadhi*,
the culmination of meditation,
all these things come by themselves,
they just happen naturally.
Since we forgot this central *sadhana*
all our efforts have been external and superficial.

True *sadhana* is not just ethical,
it is basically yoga practice.
Ethics alone are negative
and nothing enduring can be constructed on negation.
Yoga is positive and can therefore form a base.
I want to convey this positive basis to all.

1964

14.

Love.
I have received your very affectionate letter.
You write that my words ring in your ears;
what I want is for their echo to carry you
into that space where everything is silent, empty.
This is the way from words to emptiness.
There one meets *oneself*.

I am in bliss.
Take my love
I have nothing else to offer, it is my only wealth.
The marvel of it is that the more of it you give
the more it becomes.
Real wealth is like that –
it grows as you give it away;
and if it diminishes – it is not wealth at all.

Write again,
for not only do you wait for my letters,
I too wait for yours.

15.

Love.
On returning from the meditation camp
I had to leave town again.
I returned only last night but I thought of you all the time.

I cannot forget the thirst for God I saw in your eyes
and the striving for truth in your heart.
This is a blessing because no one can *attain*
without passing through this anguish.

Remember, thirst is a prerequisite
for the birth of light and love.
Together, light and love *are* God.
When love has no limits
its flame becomes smokeless and so divine.
I have seen the seeds of this growth within you
and it fills my soul with great joy.
The seed is there, now it has to become a tree.
It could be that the time is at hand.

God-realization cannot happen without meditation
so you must turn towards this now
with courage and perseverance.
I have great hopes – will you fulfill them?

My regards to other friends there.
I wait for your letter.
Remember what I said about the blank paper?
Everything else is fine.
I am in bliss.

16.

Love.
I received your letter.
What you say has made me very happy.
Words that come out of the depth and fullness of heart
echo the infinite
just as a tiny flower expresses infinite beauty.
When love breathes life into words
what is expressed is
not what is said
but what wants to be said.
Inside each of us there is a poet,
there is poetry,
but because we live on the surface
these are never born.

Those who go deep
awaken divine love
and this love fills their lives
with music, beauty, peace and poetry –
their very lives become music
and on to this stage truth descends.

Truth will descend where there is music
so life must be turned into a melody.
Only through music can one reach the truth.
You too have to become music,
the entire life, every little act,
has to be turned into music:
this happens through love.

Whatever is – love it.
Feel love for the whole world.
Feeling love for all with every breath
brings the inner music.
Have you ever seen this happen?

See this,
fill yourself with love and see.
Whatever breaks up the inner music –
that alone is irreligious, that alone is sin.
And whatever fills us with music –
that is religion, that *alone* is religion.
Love is religion
because love is beauty,
love is music.
Love is God
because it is all that is needed to attain him.

Give my love to everybody there
and feel the light of my love beside you.

17.

Love.
I have received your letter.
You long for the peace I have within me.
It is yours any time.
It is the deepest possibility in everyone,
it only has to be uncovered.
As springs of water lie hidden under layers of earth
so does bliss lie hidden within us.
The possibility is there for everyone
but only those who dig for it can redeem it.
The excavation of these hidden treasures
lies through religion.
Digging with it one reaches the well of light within.

I have shown you how to dig and what with,
but the digging has to be done by you.
I know your soil is absolutely ready,
with very little effort the infinite streams can be reached.
This state of mind is attained
with the greatest good fortune
so don't waste it or miss this opportunity.
Fill yourself with determination
and leave the rest to God.
Truth runs alongside will.

Don't hesitate to write, I have lots of time for you.
I am for those who need me –
nothing in my life is for myself.

18.

Love,
so much love.
I received your letter when I got back.
I could feel the ardor of your heart through your words.

I well know the fervor that stirs your soul
and the thirst that turns into tears within you.
I was once there too, I too have suffered it.
I can well understand your heart because I have traveled those
same paths you now have to take
in the quest for God.
I too have experienced the longing
that one day turns into a raging fire
in which one has to consume oneself.
But this burning brings the birth of a new life.
The drop can only become the ocean
when it ceases to exist.

Continue your efforts in meditation;
you have to go deeper and deeper into it –
it is the only way.
Through it and it alone can one reach life's truth.

Remember:
If you become absorbed in *sadhana*,
fully committed and surrendered,
you are bound to reach the truth.
This is an eternal law.
No step taken towards God is ever wasted.

My regards to all.

19.

My respects to you.
Your letters were received.
I have just got back from a camp at Ranakpur.
It was just for friends from Rajasthan,
that's why you weren't informed.
It lasted five days and about sixty people participated.
It was a wonderful success
and it was obvious that much happened.

Encouraged by the results
the organizers are planning a camp on an all-India basis.
You must come to that.

I am glad to hear your meditation is progressing.
You have only to be silent.
To be silent is everything.
Silence does not mean absence of speech,
it means absence of thoughts.
When the mind quietens down
it becomes linked to the infinite.
Don't do anything,
just sit and watch the flow of thoughts, just watch.
This just *watching* dissolves thought by itself.
The awakening of witnessing
brings freedom from the modifications of the mind.
With thoughts finished, consciousness is.
This is *samadhi*.

Love to all friends.

1965

20.

Love
Last night when lamps and lamps
were lit up all over town
I thought: My Sohan, too, must have lit lamps
and a few among them must surely be for me!
And then I began to see the lamps you had lit,
and also those your love has kept lit always.

I shall stay here another day.
I have talked of you to everybody
and they are eager to meet you.

21.

Beloved!
Your letter came, and your photo too.
You look really simple and innocent in it!
Such love and devotion!
The heart when purified by love turns into a temple
and I can see this clearly in your photo.
May God help this simple innocence grow!

Two thousand years ago someone asked Christ:
Who can enter the kingdom of heaven?
Jesus pointed to a little child and said:
Those whose hearts are as innocent as a child's.
Looking at your picture today, I remembered this story.

22.

Love.
I have only just arrived here, the train was five hours late.
You wanted me to write as soon as I got here
so I am doing so.
Throughout the journey I thought of you
and of the tears falling from your eyes.
Nothing in the world is more sacred
than tears of love and joy.   .
Such tears, so pure, are not of this world.
Though part of the body,
they express something which is not.
Whatever can I give you in return?

23.

Love.
I looked for your letter as soon as I got here yesterday.
Though it was Sunday, I kept waiting for it.
It came this evening –
how much you write in so few words!
When the heart is full it pours into the words
and so few are needed.
An ocean of love can be contained in just a jug!
As for scriptures on love –
it is enough to know the four letters of the word!
Do you know how many times I read
through your letters?

24.

Love.
Your letter arrived this morning.
The garland you have weaved
from flowers of love

has a fragrance that I can catch!
And the love-vine you have sown
spreads through my heart!
The tears of your love and joy
bring light and strength to my eyes!
How blissful it all is!

25.

Love.
I am in bliss.
It was good that you met me in Bombay,
my heart was overjoyed to see what is happening in you.
This is how a person prepares
and moves along the stairway towards truth.

Life is a dual journey:
one journey is in time and space
the other is within oneself and truth.
The first ends in death
the second in deathlessness.
The second is the real journey
because it takes you somewhere.
Those who take the first journey as it, waste their lives.
The real life begins the day you start the other journey.
A really good beginning
has taken place in your consciousness
and I am filled with bliss to feel this.

26.

Love.
On my return home from the tour
I looked for your letter.
It came together with the grapes
so the letter, already sweet, became still sweeter.

I am in bliss.
Your love enhances it yet more
and the love of all makes it infinite.
One body – so much bliss!
What else can others do but envy he
who feels all bodies to be his!
May God make you envious of me,
may everybody envy me,
this is my prayer.

27.

Love.
Your letter reached me
as I was sitting on that very same spot on the grass!
What I was thinking then
I shall tell you only when we meet.
What a fragrance memories leave behind!

When life is filled with love
it is so blissful.
Life's only paupers are those
without love in their hearts,
and how to describe the good fortune
of those whose hearts hold nothing but love!
In moments of such abundance
one encounters God.
Only love alone have I known as God.

28.

Love.
I received your letter.
I am blissful to learn of your bliss.
This for me is bliss.
With every breath

I pray for all to be filled with bliss.
This is my understanding of religion.

The religion that ends in temples, mosques, churches,
is a dead religion.
A religion that fails to go beyond dead words and doctrines has
no significance.
An authentic and living religion
unites one with *the whole*
and leads one to *the whole*.
Religion is whatever unites you with the cosmos.
Whatever feelings lead you towards
this marvellous meeting and merging
are prayers, and all those prayers
can be expressed in a single word;
that word is *love*.

What does love want?
Love wants to share with all
the bliss it has.
Love wants to share itself with everyone!
To give of oneself unconditionally – that is love.
To love is to dedicate
one's being to the whole
as the drop surrenders to the sea.
I pulsate with such love.
It has filled my life with nectar and light.
Now I have only one wish:
that what has happened to me should happen to all!

Give my love to everyone there.

29.

Love.
I received your letter.
How did you hurt your finger?

It sounds as if you are not taking care of your body.
And why the restless mind?
In this dreamlike world there is nothing worth making the mind
restless for.
Peace is the greatest bliss
and there is nothing worth losing it for.
Meditate on it.
Just being aware of the truth brings about inner change.

I think you won't be coming to Udaipur to assist me
and that's on your mind.
Come if you can,
if you can't – never mind;
you are helping me all the time.
Isn't one's love help enough?
If you don't come I will miss you
because the camp at Udaipur
is linked for me with being with you,
so I am hoping you can come.

Regards to all.

30.

Love.
and lots of it.
I looked at once for your letter
amongst the pile waiting for me on my return.
I can't tell you how glad I was to get it –
written by hand, too.

You write: Now your presence is felt in your absence.
Love really is presence.
Where there is love
space and time vanish,
and where there is no love
even what is near in space and time

keeps immeasurably apart.
Only lovelessness separates
and love is the only nearness.
Those who find total love
discover everything within themselves.
The whole world then is inside, not outside
and the moon and stars lie in the inner sky.
In this fullness of love, ego vanishes.
I want God to lead you to this fullness.

31.

Love.
I arrived here yesterday
and have been thinking of writing ever since
but it didn't happen until now.
Forgive the delay
though even a single day's delay is no small delay!

What shall I say about the return journey?
It was very blissful.
I kept sleeping, and you were with me.
It appeared I had left you behind
but actually you were still with me.
This is the being-together that is so real
that it cannot be divided.

Physical nearness is not nearness,
there can be no union on that level,
only an unbridgeable gulf,
but there is another nearness which is not of the body, and
name is love.
Once gained it is never lost.

Then no separation exists
despite vast distances in the visible world.
If you can arrive at this *distancelessness*

with even one other it can be found with everybody.
One is the door, the all, the goal.
The beginning of love is through one, the end is all.
The love that unites you with everything,
with nothing excluded, I call religion,
and the love that stops *anywhere* I call sin.

32.

Love.
I received your letter;
I have been waiting for it ever since I returned.
But how sweet it is to wait!
Life itself is a waiting!

Seeds wait to sprout,
rivers to reach the ocean.
What does man wait for?
He too is the seed for some tree,
a river for some ocean.

Whoever looks deep inside
finds that a longing for the endless and boundless
is his very being.
And whoever recognizes this
begins his journey towards God
because who can be thirsty and not look for water?
This has never happened and never will!
Where there is longing,
there is thirst for attainment.

I want to make everyone aware of this thirst.
I want to convert everyone's life into a waiting.
The life that has turned into a waiting for God
is the true life.
All other ways of life are just a waste, a disaster.

33.

Love.
I received your letter.
Its poetry filled my heart.
It is said that poetry is born out of love.
In your letter I saw this happen.
Where there is love
the whole existence becomes a poem;
the flowers of life bloom under the light of love.

It is strange that you ask
why my heart holds so much love for you.
Can love ever be caused?
If it is,
can it be called love?
Oh, my mad friend! love is always uncaused!
This is its mystery,
and its purity.
Love is divine
and belongs to the kingdom of God
because it is uncaused.

As for me
I am filled with love
as a lamp is filled with light.
To see this light one needs eyes.
You have those eyes so you saw the light.
The credit is yours, not mine.

34.

Love.
I never imagined that you would write
such a loving letter!
And you say that you are uneducated!
There is no knowledge greater than love,

and those who lack love – these are the true illiterates,
because the heart is the real thing in life,
not the intellect.
Bliss and light spring from the heart, not from the mind, and you
have so much heart – that is enough!
Can there be a better witness of this than me?
I am surprised that you write asking me
to point out any mistakes you have made.
So far on earth, love has not made one mistake.
All mistakes happen through lack of love,
in fact this for me is the only mistake in life.
Writing to you: May God make you envious of me
was no mistake:
I would like the bliss that has arisen in my heart
to make you thirst for it more and more.
Queen of Mewal!
there is no reason for you to worry about it!

35.

Love.
It was just this time of night, two days ago
that I left you at Chittor.
I can see now
the love and bliss filling your eyes.
The secret of all prayer and worship
is hidden in the overflow of those tears.
They are sacred.
God fills the heart of those he blesses
with tears of love,
and what to say about the calamity of those
whose hearts are filled instead with thorns of hate?

Tears flowing in love
are offerings of flowers at the feet of God
and the eyes from which they flow
are blessed with divine vision.

Only eyes filled with love can see God.
Love is the only energy
that transcends the inertia of nature
and takes one to the shores of ultimate awareness.
I think that by the time this letter reaches you
you will already have left for Kashidham.
I don't know how your journey was
but I hope it passed in song and laughter.
Give my kind respects to everyone there.
I am waiting for your promised letters.

1966

36.

Love.
I was very happy to meet you the other day.
I felt the stirrings of your heart and the longing of your soul.
You have not yet flowered as you were born to:
the seed is ready to sprout and the soil is right.
You will not have long to wait.
But now you have to work with great determination.
It is only a matter of starting the journey,
God's gravitational pull does the rest.

37.

Love.
It is good that you are forgetting the past –
it will open up an altogether new dimension of life.
To live completely in the present is freedom.
The past does not exist apart from memory
and nor does the future apart from castles in the air.
What *is, is* always present,
and if you start living unreservedly in the present
you live in God.
Once you are free of past and future
the mind turns empty and peaceful,
its waves die down
and what is left is limitless, endless.
This is the ocean of truth –
and may your river reach it!

P.S. I shall probably go to Ahmedabad in January,
can you come with me?
It would be good if we traveled together for a few days.

38.

Love.
I am glad to see such thirst for God!
To have this thirst is a divine blessing;
where there is thirst – *there the way is*.
In fact, intense longing *becomes* the way.

God is summoning us at every moment
but because the strings of our heart are slack
we don't echo his call.
If our eyes are closed then even if the sun is at the door we will
be in darkness;
and the sun is always at the door –
we only have to open our eyes and let it in, that's all!

May God give you light, that's my wish.
My love and I are always with you.

Regards to the family and love to the children.

39.

Love.
I have your letter.
The wheel of the world keeps spinning
but why spin with it?
See what is behind body and mind;
that has never moved,
is not moving,
can never move,
and thou art that, *tat twam asi*.

Waves lie on the surface of this ocean
but in its depths – what is *there*?
When the waves are taken for the ocean
it is a terrible mistake.

Look at the wheel of a bullock cart:
the wheel turns because the axle does not;
so remember your own axle,
standing, sitting, asleep or awake,
keep it in mind.
By and by, one begins to encounter
the changeless behind all change.

You have asked me about the poem.
I had a little piece read out by someone,
then it came to me: I should hear it from you yourself!
Now when you read it out to me I shall listen –
and then I can read both you and your poem.

40.

Love.
I received your letter on my return.
I welcome this birth of determination in you.
Such strength of will alone
takes us to truth.
Our deepest powers are aroused by it,
the unorganized energy becomes organized
and then there is music.

What tremendous energy exists in this atom of self!
But it can't be known without utter intensity of will.
You must have seen rocks
that even the strongest chisel cannot break,
and yet the sprouting shrub or plant
slips cracks and crevices through it so easily!
When the tiniest seed is filled with determination
to push through and reach the sun,
even the hardest rock has to give way.
So a weak seed wins over the mighty rocks!
The tender seed breaks through the hardest of rocks!
Why? Because no matter

how strong and powerful the rock,
it is dead,
and because it is dead it has no will.
The seed is tender,
it is weak,
but alive!
Remember, where there is will there is life
and where there is no will there is no life.
The seed's will becomes its power.
and with this power
its tiny roots sprout,
enter the rock and spread out,
until one day they break the rock.

Life always wins over death.
The living force within has never been defeated
by the dead obstacles without – and never will be.

41.

Love.
Your letter was received with joy.
When the heart thirsts so much
for truth,
for peace,
for religion,
one day you come face to face with the sun
which dispels all life's darkness.
Thirst!
Pray!
Strive!
Wait!
A journey of a thousand miles is covered
step by small step,
so don't lose heart.
Vast distances can be covered one step at a time
and an ocean filled drop by drop.

My regards to all.
I shall be coming soon now.
The rest when we meet.

42.

Love.
Your letter has arrived.
You ask me about sex.
That energy too belongs to God
and through meditation it too can be transformed.

No energy is bad but there can, of course,
be wrong use of energy.
When sex energy flows upwards
it turns into *brahmacharya* (godly behavior).
It is good that you are becoming detached from it
but that isn't enough.
You have to go through it to transform it,
rejection just leaves you arid and dry!

It is true you are not alone in your sex life
but sex is not essentially of the body at all
but a modification of the mind.
If the mind is completely transformed
it affects the other person too,
and one who is related so intimately
is quickly affected.

Until we meet, keep in mind that:

there should be no calculated ill-will towards sex – cultivated
detachment is useless.

Stay aware whilst making love,
be a witness in this situation;
if one can stay

in a state of meditation and right-mindfulness
then the sex energy can be successfully transformed.

We shall talk more about this when we meet.
Brahmacharya is a complete science in itself
and many doors to bliss open on that path.

Still, the very first thing is
a friendly attitude towards all one's energies.
Enmity towards them does not lead to spiritual revolution
but to self-destruction.

Give my regards to all there.
You are not coming to Poona – I shall miss you.

43.

Love.
You have asked me about the sense of humor.
We can talk about it in detail when we meet
but first of all:
the sense of humor should be directed towards oneself –
it is a very great thing to laugh at oneself
and he who can laugh at himself
gradually becomes full of concern
and compassion for others.
In the entire world no event,
no subject, invites laughter
like oneself.

About the truth of dreams as well
we shall have to talk in detail.
Some dreams are definitely true.
As the mind quietens down
glimpses of truth begin to appear in dreams.
Dreams are of four kinds
 – those concerned with past lives,

– those concerned with the future,
– those concerned with the present,
– and those concerned with repressed desires.
Contemporary psychology knows something
about the fourth type only.

I am glad to know
that your mind moves towards being at peace.
Mind is what we want it to be,
peace and restlessness are both our own creations.
Man binds himself with his own chains
and so he is always at liberty to become free of the mind.

1967

44.

Love.
What gift is greater than love?
And still you ask – What have I given?
Oh, mad one!
When love is given
there is nothing left to give,
not even the giver,
for to give love is to give oneself.
You have given yourself,
now where are you?
Having lost yourself,
now you are bound to find
the one you have been longing to meet.
Now she has been born,
and I am a witness to it,
I have watched it happen.
I can hear the music that you are going to be.
The other day, when your heart was close to me,
I heard it.
Intellect knows of the present
but for the heart the future is also the present.

1968

45.

Love.
I received your letter.
The time of my birth will have to be looked up.
I think the day was the eleventh of December,
but even this is not certain.
But tell your astrologer friend not to worry;

the future will simply come,
there's no point in worrying about it.
Whatever happens – ultimately it is all the same.
Dust returns unto dust
and life disappears like a line drawn on water.

My regards to everyone.

46.

Love.
It is a long time since I received your letter,
you must be tired of waiting for a reply.
Still, patient waiting has its own joy.
On the path to God,
timeless waiting is the true sadhana.
Waiting and waiting and waiting.
And then,
just as a bud blooms,
everything happens by itself.

You are coming to Nargol, aren't you?
My regards to all.

47.

Love.
I was glad to receive your letter.

Truth is unknown,
and to know it one has to die to the known.
Once the banks of the known are left behind
one enters the ocean of the unknown.
Be brave and take the jump!
Into emptiness, the great emptiness!
Because that's where God lives.

Love to all,
or to the only one!
For only the one is.
He alone is.
He is in all.
He is in all and in the emptiness also.

48.

Love.
I have your letter and your question.
Wherever *I* is there is a barrier;
In fact, the *I-attitude* is the one and only barrier,
so sleeping, waking, sitting, walking –
always be aware of it;
see it,
recognize it
and remember it
wherever and whenever it comes,
for recognition spells its death.
It is not the truth but just a dream,
and as soon as one becomes aware of dreaming
the dream vanishes.
Dreams cannot be renounced –
how can you give up that which is not?
To be aware of it is enough.
Ego is man's dream, his sleep,
so those who try to renounce it
fall into yet another illusion.
Their humility, their egolessness
are simply more dreams –
like dreaming you are waking whilst still dreaming.
Don't fall into this trap.
Just keep in mind one thing:
Wake up and see!

Regards to everyone there.

49.

Love.
I am so happy to have got your letter.
Can even a ray of love ever come
without the fragrance of joy?
And what is joy but the fragrance of love?
Yet the world is full of mad people
seeking happiness their whole lives –
but with their backs turned towards love!
The doors to God only open
when love turns into the prayer of our total being.
But perhaps his doors are already open,
yet eyes closed to love
will, even so, never be able to see them.

And what is this you write? *momentary contact?*
No! No! How can love's contact be so?
Love turns even a moment into eternity.
Where there is love
there is nothing momentary,
where there is love
there is eternity.
Is a drop just a drop?
No! No! It is the ocean!
The drop seen through eyes of love becomes the ocean!

50.

Love.
I have got your letter.
I know well how your soul thirsts;
soon it can be quenched –
you are right at the brink of the lake.
You only have to open your eyes,
and I can see that the lids are about to lift.
I shall be with you then,

always with you,
so don't worry.
Be patient and wait;
the seed takes its own time to break and bloom.

Give my regards to all.
More when we meet.

51.

Love.
I have received your letter and your questions.
About death I have remained quiet on purpose,
because I want to awaken inquiry about life.
Those who ponder over death reach nowhere.
Because, in fact, how can death be known without dying?
Hence, the total outcome of such thinking is either a belief that
the soul is immortal or that the end of one's life is a total end,
nothing remains after that.
They are both mere beliefs.
One belief is based on the fear of death,
the other on the end of the body.
I want man not to get entangled in beliefs and opinions,
because that is not the direction to experiencing,
to knowing.
And what else can be found by thinking about death
but belief systems and dogmas?
Thought never takes one beyond the known.
And death is unknown.
Hence, it cannot be known through thinking.
I want to turn your attention towards life.
Life is – here and now.
One can enter it.
Death is never here and now –
either it is in the future or in the past.
Death is never in the present.
Has this fact ever come to your attention,

that death is never in the present?
But life is always in the present –
neither in the past nor in the future.
If it is, it is now; otherwise it never is.
Hence it can be known, because it can be lived,
there is no need to think about it.
In fact, those who would think about it will miss it.
Because the movement of thought is also only of the past
or in the future;
thought is not in the present.
Thought too is a companion of death.
In other words, thought is dead,
there is no element of life in it.
Aliveness is always in the present – it is the present.
Its manifestation is now, absolutely now;
here, absolutely here.
Hence, there is no thinking about life,
there is only experiencing.
Not an experience, but experiencing.
Experience means, it has already happened;
experiencing means, it is happening.
Experience has already become a thought,
because it has already happened.
Experiencing is thoughtless:
wordless – silent – void.
Hence I call thoughtless awareness
the door to experiencing life.
And the one who comes to know life comes to know all.
He comes to know death as well
because death is nothing but a fallacy
born out of not knowing life.
One who does not know life
naturally believes himself to be the body.
And the body dies, the body is destroyed;
the entity called body disappears.
It is this that gives birth to the concept
that death is a total end.
Only those who are a little more courageous

accept this concept.

It is also out of this very fallacy of believing oneself
to be the body that the fear of death is born.
It is the people suffering this fear who start chanting,
"the soul is immortal, the soul is immortal."
The fearful and weak seek refuge in this way.
But both these concepts
are born out of one and the same fallacy.
These are two forms of the same fallacy
and are two different reactions of two types of people.
But, remember, the fallacy of both is the same,
and in both ways it is the same fallacy
that is strengthened.
I do not want to give any kind of support to this fallacy.
If I say the soul is not immortal, then that is an untruth.
If I say the soul is immortal,
then that becomes an escape from your fear.
And those who are in fear
are never able to know the truth.
Hence, I say death is unknown.
Know life. Only that can be known.
And upon knowing that, immortality is also known.
Life is eternal.
There is no beginning and no end to it.
It manifests, it unmanifests.
It moves from one form to another form.
In our ignorance,
these transition points of change look like death.
But for one who knows,
death is nothing more than changing houses.
Certainly there is rebirth;
but for me it is not a doctrine, it is an experience.
And I don't want to make it a doctrine for others either.
Doctrines have badly undermined the truth.
I want every person to know it for themselves.
Nobody can perform this act for the other.
But, through doctrines,
it is this very act that appears to have been accomplished,

thus everybody's individual search
has become dull and dead.
Believing in the doctrines and scriptures
one has sat down quietly,
as if one has neither to know anything for oneself,
nor has to do anything about finding the truth.
This situation is utterly suicidal.
Hence, I don't want to participate
in this vast scale arrangement
for killing man through the repetition of doctrines.
I want to displace all the established doctrines,
because this alone seems compassionate to me.
This way, all that is untrue will be destroyed.
And the truth is never destroyed,
it is ever available in its eternal freshness
to those who seek.

52.

Love.
I received your letter.
I am always with you.
Don't be worried,
don't be sad,
and leave your *sadhana* in the hands of God.
Let his will be done.
Be like a dry leaf,
let the winds take you where they will.
Isn't this what is meant by *shunya* (nothingness)?
Do not swim,
just float.
Isn't this what is meant by *shunya?*

My regards to all.

1969

53.

Love.
Your letter has come.
Love has not to be asked for –
it is never obtained by asking.
Love comes through giving –
it is our own echo.

You feel my love pouring on you
because you have become a river of love
flowing towards me,
and when your love flows like this towards all
you will find the whole world
flowing in love towards you.

To respond with unconditional love towards all,
towards that which is,
is the God-experience.

54.

Love.
Can two people ever meet?
It is just not possible on this earth,
communication seems impossible –
but at times the impossible happens.
The other day it did.

Being with you, I felt meeting *is* possible,
and also communication,
and without words, too.
Your tears answered me.
I am deeply grateful for those tears.

Such response is very rare.

I have seen your *Madhu Shala*,
seen it again and again.
If I could sing
I would sing the same song that is there.
I call that sannyas the real *sannyas*
which accepts the world with joy.
Aren't *samsara* and *moksha* really one?
Duality exists in ignorance,
in knowledge there is only one.
Oh, can that really be religion
which cannot sing and dance the songs of bliss and love?

P.S. I hear you are due to come here.
Come, and come soon.
Who can trust time?
Look – it is morning and the sun rises.
How long will it be before it sets?

55.

Love.
I am one with all things –
in beauty, in ugliness,
for whatsoever is, there I am.
Not only in virtue
but in sin too I am a partner;
and not only heaven but hell too is mine.
Buddha, Jesus, Lao Tzu –
it is easy to be their heir.
But Chenghis, Taimur and Hitler?
They are also within me!
No, not half – *I am the whole of mankind!*
Whatsoever is man's is mine –
flowers and thorns,
darkness as well as light.

And if nectar is mine, whose is poison?
Nectar and poison – both are mine.
Whoever experiences this I call religious,
for only the anguish of such experience
can revolutionize life on earth.

56.

Love.
I have received your letter.
I was very glad indeed to get it, more so since you have sent a
blank sheet.
But I have read in it all that you have not written
but wanted to write.
Besides, what can words say?
Even after writing,
what you had meant to write remains unwritten.
So your silent letter is very lovely.
As it is, whenever you come to see me you are mostly silent, but
your eyes tell all, and your silence too.
Some deep thirst has touched you, some unknown shore has
called you.
Whenever God calls he calls this way –
but how long will you go on standing on the shore?
Look! The sun is out·
and the winds can't wait to fill the boat's sails!

57.

Love.
I have received your letters – but they are not just letters really,
they are poems born out of love, out of love and prayer,
for where there is love there is prayer.
So it is possible to get glimpses of God through another
whom one loves –
love providing the eyes that can see God.

Love is the door through which he appears.
So when one loves all *he* can be seen in all things.
Part and whole in fact are not in opposition: deep love for
even one other finally spreads to all
because love dissolves the self, leaving the no-self.

Love is like the sun, the individual like frozen ice.
Love's sun melts the icebergs, leaving a limitless ocean.
So the search for love is really the search for God,
because love melts, and also destroys;
because love *only* melts and *only* destroys.

It is both birth and death.
In it the self dies and the all is born.
So there is certainly pain —
in the birth as well as in the death.
Love is the deep anguish of birth as well as death.
But the poetry flowering in you shows that you have begun to
experience the joy that lies in love's anguish.

58.

Love.
Your letter has filled my heart with joy.
You are at the threshold of a great revolution; now, even if you
want to run away I will not let you.
You will certainly have to perish in it
so that you can be reborn.

Gold has to pass through fire — only then is it purified.
Love is fire for you, and I pray to God
that your ego burns in it.
Then if love comes, prayer can come too; without love prayer is
not possible.

Remember that body and soul are not two.
The part of the person that can be seen is the body,

the part that cannot be seen is the soul.
The same holds true for God and matter: God made visible is
matter, and what cannot be seen is God.

Take life easily and naturally, just as it comes.
Welcome it in its endless forms with an attitude of complete
acceptance.
And do not impose yourself on life; life has its own discipline, its
own wisdom,
and those who are ready to live totally
have no need for any other discipline or wisdom.

But you have always been afraid of life
and therefore you are afraid of love.

Now life has begun penetrating you,
breaking your walls of security.
So, God's infinite grace showers on you!
Don't run from it now, accept it gratefully
and my good wishes are always with you.

59.

Love.
Be aware in the waking state,
don't try to become aware in sleep or dreams.
If you become aware in the waking state awareness in dreams
and sleep comes easily – but you don't have to do anything for
it. Doing only creates difficulties.

Sleep reflects the waking state:
what we are when awake we are in sleep.
If we are asleep in the waking state only then is sleep really
sleep; the stream of thoughts during the waking state becomes
the web of dreams in sleep.
Being aware in the waking state will begin to reflect itself in
sleep too, and if there are no thoughts in the waking state

dreams disappear altogether in sleep.

Everything else is fine.
My regards to everyone there.

60.

Love.
I was overjoyed to receive your letter –
as pure and innocent as your heart.
You want to write that which cannot be written
so you send an unwritten letter.
This is good, for it is better to remain silent
about that which cannot be expressed.
But beware, silence also speaks,
it speaks and speaks so much!
Silence can speak even where words fail.

The void envelops even that which lines cannot contain.
In fact what can resist the embrace of the great void?
Nothing is left unsaid by silence.

Where words fail, silence is full of meaning.
Where form ends, the formless begins.
Where knowledge (veda) ends,
transcendental knowledge (vedanta) begins.
When knowledge dies, the beyond begins.
Freedom from the word is truth.

61.

Love.
How can I describe how happy I am
to have received your letter?
Whenever I saw you,
only one question arose in my mind –

How long are you going to keep away from me?
I knew you had to come closer to me, it was only a matter of
time, so I kept waiting and praying for you.
To me, prayerful waiting is love.

I also knew you were going through the pangs of a new birth
and that rebirth is very near –
for only this can give soul to your songs.

Words are the form and form has its own beauty,
its own melody, its own music.
But this is not enough,
and he who considers this enough
remains discontented forever.
The soul of poetry lies in silence.

To me, prayerful waiting is love,
and the void is the door to the divine temple.
You have come to me and I want to take you to the Lord for
how can you come close to me
without first coming closer to him?
In fact without coming close to him
you cannot come close even to yourself.
Then as soon as you come near him
you attain that life
for which you have gone through so many lives.
To come close to oneself is to be reborn –
the principle of being twice born is just this.
And remember, not even the pebbles lying on the road
are just pebbles; they too await a new birth,
for that second birth turns them into diamonds.

P.S. To run after desires is to run after a mirage.
It is a journey from one death to another.
In the illusion that is life
man dies this way time and time again.
But those willing to die to their desires
discover that death itself dies for them.

62.

Love.
Where is truth?
Do not search for it, for when has truth
ever been found through seeking?
For in seeking, the seeker is present.
So don't seek but lose yourself.
He who loses himself finds truth.
I don't say: *Seek and you will find.*
I say: *He who loses himself, finds.*

63.

Love.
I was happy to receive your letter.
The drop doesn't have to become the ocean.
It already is the ocean,
it just has to *know* it.
What is,
however it is –
to know it as it is,
is truth.
And truth liberates.

64.

Love.
Life is an infinite mystery,
therefore those who are filled with knowledge
are deprived of life.
Life becomes known only to the innocent,
to those whose intuition is not covered
with the dust of knowledge.

65.

Love.
Do not seek *nirvana* as something opposed to life,
rather, turn life itself into *nirvana*.
Those who know, do this.
Dogen has these beautiful words to say:
Do not strive after *moksha* (liberation);
rather, allow all your actions to become liberating.
This happens.
I can tell you this from my own experience;
and the day it happens
life becomes as beautiful as a flower in full bloom
and brims with fragrance.

66.

Love.
I received your letter on my return.
Just as the seed within the soil waits for the rains
so you wait for God.

Prayerful, wholehearted surrender is the door
leading to him.
Let yourself go completely,
just like a boat floating on the river.
You do not have to row the boat, just let it go loose.
You are not to swim, just to float,
then the river itself takes you to the ocean.
The ocean is very near –
but only for those who float but do not swim.
Do not be afraid of drowning
because that fear makes you swim –
and the truth is that
he who drowns himself in God is saved forever.
And do not have a goal,
for he who has a goal begins to swim.

Remember always –
wherever one reaches, that is the destination,
therefore he who makes God his goal goes astray.
Wherever the mind is free from all goals –
there alone is God.

67.

Love.
I say: Die, so that you can live!
When the seed destroys itself, it becomes the tree;
when the drop loses itself, it becomes the ocean.
But man – man refuses to lose himself.
How then can God manifest in him?
Man is the seed, God is the tree.
Man is the drop, God is the ocean.

68.

Love.
Leave the old track –
only the dead walk on trodden paths.
Life is the continuous quest for the new.
Only he who has the knack of being new
every moment truly lives.
Die to the old every moment
so that you are forever new –
this is the crux of the transformation of life.

69.

Love.
Truth is like the sky: eternal, everlasting, boundless.
Is there a door to enter the sky?
Then how can there be one to enter into truth?

If our eyes are closed, the sky exists not.
The same holds good for truth.
Opening the eyes is the door to truth; to close the eyes
is to close that door to truth.

70.

Love.
Where to find truth?
Well, it has to be sought within one's own self,
within one's own self
within one's own self
within one's own self.
It is definitely there.
One who seeks it elsewhere loses it.

71.

Love.
I am extremely grateful for your loving letter.

I take life as *a whole* and I am incapable of viewing it in bits
and pieces; it is *already the whole* but because it has been
viewed in fragments for so long
it has become perverted.

There is no politics, no morality, no religion; there is *life*,
there is God, whole and unfragmented.
It has to be sought, recognized and lived in all its forms,
therefore I shall continue to speak on all its forms.
And this is only the beginning.
Answering journalists is just preparing the ground.
All paths lead to one end – certain friends might take some time
to understand this truth.
As things are, this delay in understanding the truth
is unavoidable, but seekers of truth won't be afraid –

courage is the first condition in the search for truth.

Remember, as long as spirituality does not become a philosophy *of the whole life* it proves impotent, and only escapists will take shelter behind it.
Spirituality has to be turned into a force, spirituality has to be turned into a revolution, only then can spirituality be saved.

My regards to all.

72.

Love.
Man becomes a slave because he is afraid to be alone,
so he needs a crowd, a society, an organization.

Fear is the basis of all institutions,
and how can a frightened mind know the truth?
Truth requires fearlessness
and fearlessness comes from *sadhana*, not from societies.
That is why all religions, institutions and organization
bar the path of truth.

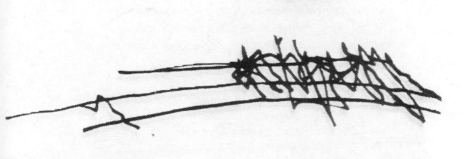

1970

73.

Love.
Don't be in a hurry.
So often, hurrying causes delay.
As you thirst, wait patiently – the deeper the waiting,
the sooner it comes.

You have sown the seed,
now sit in the shade and watch what happens.
The seed will break, it will blossom,
but you cannot speed up the process.
Doesn't everything need time?
Work you must, but leave the results to God.
Nothing in life is ever wasted,
especially steps taken towards truth.

But at times impatience comes,
impatience comes with thirst,
but this is an obstacle.
Keep the thirst and throw away the impatience.

Do not confuse impatience with thirst.
With thirst there is yearning but no struggle.
With impatience there is struggle but no yearning.
With longing there is waiting but no demanding.
With impatience there is demanding but no waiting.
With thirst there are silent tears.
With impatience there is a restless struggle.
Truth cannot be attacked; it is attained through surrender
not through struggle.
It is conquered through total surrender.

74.

Love.
Your letter has been received.

Why seek at all for a purpose?
If you seek this you will never find it
because it is eternally hidden in the seeker.

Life is without purpose – life is its own purpose,
therefore he who lives without purpose truly lives.
Live! Isn't living itself enough?

The desire to have more than just life
is a result of not properly living –
and that is why the fear of death grips the human mind,
for what is death to one who is really alive!
Where living is intense and total there is no time to fear death –
and there is no time for death, either.

Do not think in the language of *purpose* –
that language is diseased in itself.
The sky exists without purpose.

God is without purpose,
flowers bloom without purpose,
and stars shine without purpose –
what has happened to poor man
that he cannot live without purpose!

Because man can think he gets into trouble.
A little thinking always leads to trouble.
If you must think, think completely, utterly!
Then the mind whirls so fast with thoughts
that freedom from thoughts is attained.
Then you begin to live.

75.

Love.
Rest is the supreme goal, work is the medium.
Total relaxation, with complete freedom from effort,
is the supreme goal.
Then life is a play, and then even effort becomes play.

Poetry, philosophy, religion are the fruits of repose.
This has not been available to everyone,
but technology and science will make it so
in the near future.
That is why I am in favor of technology.

Those who attribute intrinsic value to labor
oppose the use of machines – they have to.
For me, labor has no such intrinsic value:
on the contrary, I see it as a burden.
As long as work is a prerequisite for rest
it cannot be blissful.
When work flows out of a state of rest voluntarily,
then it is blissful.
So I cannot call rest a sin.

Nor do I support sacrifice.
I do not want anyone to live for anybody else,
or one generation to sacrifice itself for another.
Such sacrifices turn out to be very costly –
those who make them expect an inhuman return.
This is why fathers expect the impossible
from their sons.
If each father lives for his son who will live for himself?
For every son is a potential father.
No, I want everyone to live for himself –
for his own happiness, his own state of rest.

When a father is happy he does much more for his son –
and easily, because it comes out of his happiness.

Then there is neither sacrifice nor renunciation;
what he does comes naturally out of his being a father –
and a happy father at that.
Then he has no inhuman expectations of his son,
and where there is no pressure from expectations, expectations
are fulfilled – out of the son being a son.

In short, I teach each person to be selfish.
Altruistic teachings have taught man nothing but suicide,
and a suicidal man is always homicidal.
The unhappy sow their sorrow amongst others.

I am also against the sacrifice of the present for the future,
because what is is always present.
If you live in it totally the future will be born out of it –
and when it comes it too will be the present.
For he who has the habit of sacrificing the present for the future,
the future never comes because whatever comes
is again always sacrificed for that which has not yet come.

Finally, you ask why I too work for others and for the future.
First of all, I do not work.
Whatever I do flows out of my state of rest.
I do not swim, I just float.
No one can ever do anything for another
but if something *happens* to others out of what I am,
that is something else, and there too I am not the doer.

As for the future –
for me, the present is everything.
And the past too is also a present – that has passed away.
And the future too – that is a present that is yet to come.
Life is always here and now
so I do not bother about past and future.
And it is amazing that ever since I stopped worrying about them
they have begun to worry about me!

My regards to all there.

76.

Love.
There is a music which has no sound;
the soul is restless for such silent music.
There is a love in which the body is not;
the soul longs for such unembodied love.
There is a truth which has no form;
the soul longs for this formless truth.

Therefore melodies do not satisfy,
bodies do not satisfy,
and forms cannot fulfill the soul.

But this lack of fulfillment,
this dissatisfaction, has to be understood properly,
for such understanding
ultimately brings about transcendence.

Then sound becomes the door to the soundless,
the body becomes the path to the unembodied,
and form becomes the formless.

77.

Love.
God is our only wealth.
Do not depend on any other wealth,
riches of any other kind bring only disaster.

St. Theresa wanted to set up a large orphanage
but at the time she had only three shillings.
She wanted to start this enormous project
with just this small amount.
Friends and admirers advised her:
Get the funds together first.
What can you do with just three shillings?

Theresa laughed and said:
Naturally Theresa can do nothing with three shillings,
but with three shillings plus God – nothing is impossible!

78.

Love.
Samsara is nirvana,
sound is mantra,
and all living beings are God.

It depends on how you look.
The world is nothing but how one sees it.
See! Open your eyes and see!
Where is darkness?
  – there is only light.
Where is death?
  – there is only deathlessness.

79.

Love.
I have received your letter.
As the earth thirsts for the rains after a hot summer
so you are thirsting for God.
This thirst becomes an invitation to the divine clouds –
and the invitation has arrived.
Just keep drowning yourself in meditation
and his grace will definitely pour on you.
If you are ready here –
he is always ready there.
Look! Can't you see his clouds hovering in the sky?

80.

Love.
Do not fight with yourself.
You are as you are —
do not strive to change.

Do not swim in life,
just float
like a leaf on the stream.
Keep away from *sadhanas*, mere *sadhanas*.
This is the only *sadhana*.

Where is there to go?
What is there to become?
What is there to find?
What is, is here and now.
Please, stop and see!

What are the animal instincts?
What is low? and high?
Whatever is, is — there is no high, no low.
What is animal?
What is divine?

So do not condemn, do not praise,
nor condemn nor praise yourself:
all differences are of the mind.

In truth no differences exist.
There, God and animal are one and the same;
heaven and hell are just two sides of one coin;
samsara and nirvana are two expressions of one unknown.

And do not think about what I have said;
if you think you will miss.

See. Just see.

81.

Love.
On the road to God the only sustenance is infinite hope
– hope shining like the north star in darkness,
hope keeping you company like a shadow in loneliness.
Dark and lonely life's path certainly is –
but only for those without hope.

The famous geographical explorer Donald Macmillan
was preparing for his journey to the north pole
when he received a letter.
On it was written:
To be opened only when there is no hope of survival.
Fifty years passed; the envelope remained with Macmillan as it
was – sealed.
Someone asked him the reason for this and he replied:
For one thing I want to keep faith with the unknown sender, and
for another, I have never given up hope.

What priceless words! – *I have never given up hope!*

82.

Love.
I am delighted you have taken *sannyas*.
A life without the flower of *sannyas* is like a barren tree.
Sannyas is the supreme music of life.
It is not renunciation,
on the contrary, it is life's highest enjoyment.
Someone who finds diamonds and pearls
is not going to bother about pebbles and stones.
But note – he does not renounce them,
interest simply drops away.

83.

Love.
Thought is man's strength
but blind belief has robbed him of it,
that is why he has become weak and impotent.
Think fully,
think tirelessly,
for amazingly enough the state of no-thought
is achieved only at the peak of thought,
it is the culmination of thought,
and at this point all thought becomes useless.
In this emptiness, truth lies.

84.

Love.
All crutches bar the way.
Shun all support and then you will receive his.
He is the only help for the helpless.
There is no other guide but him – all other guides are obstacles
on the path.
If you want to reach the master avoid all teachers.

Don't be afraid to make yourself empty
for that alone is the door,
that alone is the path –
and that alone is the destination.

The courage to be empty
is all that is needed to become one with the all.

Those who are full stay empty,
and those who are empty become filled –
such are his mathematics.

Do not consider doing anything –

through doing you can never reach him,
nor through chanting, nor through austerity,
for he is already here!
Stop and see!

To do is to run, not to do is to halt.
Yes! If he were far away we could run to meet him,
but he is the nearest of the near!
If we had lost him we could search for and find him,
but to us he has never been lost!

85.

Love.
I am glad to have received your letter.
The I is not to be given up because
how can you drop that which is not?
The I has to be looked into, understood.
It is like taking a lamp to search for darkness –
the darkness vanishes!
Darkness cannot be stamped out because it doesn't exist.
You just have to bring a light and darkness is unmasked.
It is the same with your thoughts – do not fight with them.
The effort to be free of thought
comes itself from a thought.
Know your thoughts, watch them, be aware of them,
then they quieten down without difficulty.
Witnessing finally leads to emptiness,
and where there is emptiness – there is the all.

86.

Love.
Why does man suffer so much?
Because in his life there is pandemonium
but no soundless music.

Because in his life there is a babble of thoughts
but no emptiness.
Because in his life there is a turmoil of feeling
but no equanimity.
Because in his life there is a mad rushing around
but no stillness which knows no directions.
And finally, because in his life there is much of himself
but of God, nothing at all.

87.

Love.
The time is ripe.
The hour draws nearer every day.
Innumerable souls are restless.
A path has to be created for them.
So hurry!
Work hard!
Surrender totally!
Forget yourself!

Plunge into God's work like a madman.
Here, only madness will do –
and there is no greater wisdom
than such madness for God.

88.

Love.
Non-attachment is not concerned with things
but with thoughts.
Non-attachment is not related to the outside
but to the within.
Non-attachment is not to do with the world
but with oneself.

One day a beggar went to see a Sufi fakir and found him seated
on a velvet cushion inside a beautiful tent with its ropes tied to
golden pegs.

Seeing all this the beggar cried: What is this!
Honorable Fakir, I have heard much about your spirituality and
non-attachment, but I am completely disillusioned by all this
ostentation around you.

The fakir laughed, replying:
I am ready to leave all this behind and come with you.
So saying, he immediately got up and walked off
with the beggar not even waiting to put his sandals on!

After a short while the beggar became distressed.
I left my begging bowl in your tent, he said.
What shall I do without it?
Please wait here while I go and fetch it.

The Sufi laughed. My friend, he said,
the gold pegs of my tent were stuck in the earth
not in my heart,
but your begging bowl is still chasing after you!

To be in the world is not attachment.
The presence of the world in the mind is the attachment, and
when the world disappears from the mind –
this is non-attachment.

89.

Love.
Once the ego is surrendered there is no suffering, no sorrow,
for the ego is basically the cause of all suffering,
and the moment it is seen that everything is God
there is no more cause for complaint.
Where complaining has ended, there is prayer.

It is a feeling of gratitude, it is trust in God.
In this trust in God, benediction pours.
Trust and know.
It is very difficult to trust – there is no austerity greater than
accepting life as it is.

90.

Love.
Do not look for results in meditation –
this is an obstruction.
Do not seek to repeat any meditative experience,
for this too is a hindrance.
When meditating, just meditate;
the rest then happens by itself.
The way to God does not lie in our hands
so leave yourself in his.
Surrender, surrender, surrender!
Remember always – surrender!
Sleeping or waking – remember!
Surrender is the only door to God.
Emptiness is the only boat that sails to him.

91.

Love.
How much longer will you go on
letting your energy sleep?
How much longer are you going to stay oblivious
of the immensity of your self?
Don't waste time in conflict,
lose no time in doubt –
time can never be recovered,
and if you miss an opportunity
it may take many lives before another
comes your way again.

92.

Love.
I received your letter.
Do not fall into the whirl of calming the mind;
this in itself is the restlessness.
The mind is what it is, accept it as such.
This acceptance brings peace.

Rejection is restlessness, acceptance is peace –
and he who reaches total acceptance attains to God.
There is no way other than this.

Understand this well
because this understanding brings acceptance.
Acceptance cannot come from an act of will – .
the action of will is itself non-accepting.
I do conceals non-acceptance
because will is always of the ego.
Ego cannot live unless fed by rejection.
Acceptance can never be brought about by action,
only understanding life can bring it about.

Look, look at life.
What is *is*, it is as it is.
Things are such – do not ask for them to be otherwise because
they cannot be even if you so desire.
Desire is altogether impotent.
Ah, how can there be restlessness without desire?

93.

Love.
Search, search and search –
so much that finally the seeker vanishes.
There you meet him.
Where the I is lost, there he is.

There is not, and never has been,
any wall between –
except for the *I*.

94.

Love.
When the moon rises in the sky watch it, be absorbed by it –
forget everything else, including yourself!
Only then will you come to know
the music that has no sound.
When the morning sun rises,
bow down to the earth and lose yourself in homage to it.
Only then will you know of the music
that is not made by man.
When the trees burst into flowers,
like a flower dance with them in the breeze.
Only then will you hear the music
that lives in one's innermost self.
He who knows this music knows life too – its song
is another word for God.

95.

Love.
Don't float with the current of thoughts,
just be aware of them.
Know that you are separate from them,
distinct, distant, just an observer.
Just watch the flow of thoughts like traffic,
watch them as you watch the dry leaves
flying everywhere in the fall.
Don't be the one who makes them happen,
don't be the one to whom they happen.
Then the rest takes place by itself.
This rest is what I call meditation.

96.

Love.
This is a good beginning to the struggle
and I am glad to have pushed you into it.
Sannyas is a challenge to the world,
a fundamental declaration of freedom.
To live in freedom every moment is _sannyas_.
Now, insecurity will always be with you,
but that is a fact of life.

The only certainty is death; life is insecurity,
and that is its joy and its beauty.
To be locked in security is suicide,
a living death effected by one's own hand.

Such living-dead are everywhere.
They have turned the world into a graveyard,
and they number amongst them many celebrated corpses.
They all have to be awakened,
though for their part they are trying to put back to sleep
even those who are awake.

Now the struggle will go on and on.
In it your total resolution _will_ be born.
Far off I see your destination – the other shore.

97.

Love.
I was traveling, then on my return, there was your letter.

You can meet friends of Jeevan Jagruti Kendra and begin
working for Yuvak Kranti Dal (Revolutionary Youth Force).
There are no rules about it –
there can never be rules in revolution.
There needs to be an awakening of understanding among the

youth, with scientific studies replacing blind faith –
this is all I wish for.

Do meet me this time when I come to Indore.
Everything is fine.
My regards to everyone there.

98.

Love.
My work is only God's work;
apart from this there is neither me nor mine.

No other work exists apart from his.
You just live in God, that's all,
and the rest happens by itself.

Jesus said: First seek ye the Kingdom of God,
then all else will be added unto you.
I say the same.
But the mind of man seeks all else first,
so what is bound to happen, happens –
nothing else is gained.
and he even loses whatever he had.

99.

Love.
The fragrance of *sannyas*
has to be spread around the world.
Religions, like gaols,
have imprisoned the flower of *sannyas* too
within their great walls.
Hence the *sannyasin* has to say now:
I belong to no religion – all religions are mine.
It was a terrible mistake

to tear *sannyas* away from the world.
It has.become bloodless.
And the world without sannyas has lost its life.
A new bridge has to be built between the two.
Sannyas has to be given back its blood,
and the world, its soul.
Sannyas has to be returned to *samsara,*
fearless and unattached:
in the world yet not of it,
in the crowds, yet alone!

And the world has to be brought to *sannyas* too,
fearless and unattached.
Then *sannyas* will be a real *sannyas*
and not an escape from the world.
It will be *sannyas* and in the world.
Only then can that bridge of gold be built
joining the seen with the unseen,
the form with the formless.
Commit yourself to this great work,
join in the building of this great bridge!

100.

Love.
Even the impossible is not impossible if resolution is there,
and even the possible becomes impossible
if one lacks will.
The world we live in is our own creation.

The time gap between sowing and reaping creates confusion.
Because cause and effect are so separated the mind fails to
understand what would otherwise be obvious.
Nothing is fragmented or disconnected.
The missing links are always there if you look deeply.
Understanding the life process opens the door to peace.
The light lies close by, waiting for the seeker.

101.

Love.
I am glad to receive your letter.
You have the strength within
but you don't know about it.
To find it you need a catalyst.
The day you realize all this you will laugh,
but until then I am prepared to be your catalyst.
I am already laughing and just waiting
for the day you can join
in this cosmic laughter.

See! Krishna is laughing! Buddha is laughing!
Listen! The earth and heaven are laughing!
But man is weeping for he doesn't know what he is.
What a joke! What a game!
Emperors go on begging and fish in the ocean
are thirsty !

102.

Love.
Existence is a play of sun and shade
of hope and despair,
of happiness and sorrow,
of life and death.
So existence is duality –
a tension of opposite poles,
a music of contrary notes.

To know it,
to recognize it,
to experience it as such,
is to go beyond it.
This transcendence is the real *sadhana*,
the real achievement.

The key to this transcendence
is the witness state.
Bid goodbye to the doer,
live in the witness state.
Watch the drama.
Don't drown in it,
rather be drowned in observing.
Then happiness and sorrow,
birth and death,
remain just a play;
they do not affect you,
they cannot affect you.

All error, all ignorance, comes from identification.

103.

Love.
I received your letter.
It is good to know that your mother's death
has made you consider your own.
One has to go through the awareness of death
to reach deathlessness.

The thrust of death goes deep
but the mind cunningly goes on evading it.
Don't evade it,
don't console yourself –
any kind of consolation is a suicide.
Let yourself feel the wound of death completely:
wake up and live with it!
This will be hard
but revolution always is.

Death is,
it is there always,
but we forget about it.

Every day death is there,
every moment.

104.

Love.
I received your letter.
So many questions!
To answer them I would have to write a book
bigger than the *Mahabharata!*
But even then you would not get your answers
because some questions others can never answer –
your answers lie deep within your own life.
And some questions have no answers
because they are wrong questions
for which no answers can be found.
As the search continues
these questions always gradually drop away.
Then there are some questions which are right questions
but have no answers at all.
They have to be *experienced* deep within oneself.

105.

Love.
Do not desire bliss
because that desire gets in the way.
Live life unchained to desire
and without an eye on a goal.
Live *free!*
Live from moment to moment!
And don't be afraid, be free of fear
because there is nothing to lose –
and nothing to gain

– and the moment you realize this
the totality of life is attained.
But never approach the gates of life as a beggar,
never go begging,
for those gates never open to beggars!

106.

Love.
It brings me happiness to bear witness to your new birth.
You have worked for it over many lives
and now the boat flows rightly,
I can rest assured about you.
Once I made you a promise and this is now fulfilled.
It is your turn to fulfill your part of the promise;
make sure you don't miss the chance.
Time is short
and I may not be able to be with you again.
Muster your whole will, take the oars in your hands
and begin the journey that is infinite.
You have wasted much time sitting on the banks;
now the winds are favorable.
This I know,
and that's why I am pushing you off
the banks so earnestly.
God's grace is showering –
be open to it and let it in.
Dance it and drink it in!
With such nectar at hand will you still stay thirsty?

107.

Love.
What is sought totally is always attained.
Thoughts, when concentrated,
become things.

As the river finds the ocean;
thirsty souls find the temple of God.
But the thirst must be intense
and the work tireless
and the waiting without end
and the calling with the whole heart.
And all this thirst, work, waiting, calling –
are contained in one small word
and that word is prayer.
But praying cannot be performed,
it is not an act,
you can only be in it.
It is a feeling,
it is the soul,
it is a surrender of oneself
without words or demands.
Leave yourself to the unknown
and accept whatever comes.
Whatever God makes of you – accept it,
and if he breaks you, accept that too.

108.

Love
My blessings on your new birth
 – *sannyas* is a new birth,
in oneself, by oneself, of oneself.
It is also a death,
not an ordinary death but *the great death*.
It is the death of all that you were up until yesterday.
And what you are now –
that too must keep dying every moment
so that the new can be born and born and born again.
Now you will not remain you even for a moment.
You have to die and be reborn every moment –
this is the only *sadhana*.
Live like a river, not like a pond.

The pond is a householder;
the river, a sannyasin.

109.

Love.
The temple of God is open only
to a dancing, singing, happy heart.
A sad heart cannot enter there
so avoid sadness.
Fill your heart with color
as vivid as a peacock –
and for no reason.
He who has reason to be happy is not really happy.
Dance and sing –
not for others,
not for a reason,
just dance for dancing's sake;
sing for singing's sake;
then one's whole life becomes divine
and only then becomes prayer.
To live so is to be free.

110.

Love.
I am glad to get your letter.
The moment of the inward revolution is near
but first you have to go through the birth pangs.
Nothing hurts more than this giving birth to oneself
but what comes after it is life's greatest bliss.
So, longing, waiting, prayer –
take these for your _sadhana_.

Everything else is fine.
My regards to all.

111.

Love.
As the birds sing each morning at sunrise,
the heart fills with song at the dawn of meditation.
As flowers bloom in spring,
the soul is drenched in fragrance.
as meditation is born.
As everything glistens green beneath the rain,
consciousness shines with many colors
as meditation showers.
All this and much more takes place,
and this is only the beginning.
Ultimately everything goes;
fragrance, color, light, music –
everything disappears.
And an inner space, like the sky, appears –
empty, formless, without quality.
Wait for that. Long for that.
The signs are good, so do not waste even a moment.
Go on! I am always with you.

112.

Love.
Thirst is good,
longing is good, an aching heart is good,
because he comes through the vale of tears.
Weep so much
that only the tears remain, not you.
If the tears alone remain
and he who weeps vanishes
then God comes by himself.

That is why I let you go, not stopping you.
I knew you would regret it –
but this regret is good.

I knew you would weep
but these tears have their usefulness –
can there be a profounder prayer than tears?

113.

Love.
What is truth?
This much at least can be said:
It cannot be defined.
So forget about all definitions,
drop all evaluations and interpretations –
these are all mind games,
all creatures of thought.
What is, is beyond the mind.

Thoughts are as unaware of reality
as the waves are of the peace of the lake.
With waves
the lake loses its tranquility;
when the lake is calm
then the waves cannot exist.
One has to know that-which-is.
Its interpretation is very different from knowing it.
Interpretations take one astray –
they are as illusory as scarecrows.
The seeker of truth has to be wary of words.
Words are not the truth,
truth cannot be words.
Truth is an experience,
truth is reality,
and the path to it is neti, neti –
neither this nor that.

Drop explanations,
drop definitions,
drop scriptures and doctrines,

remember *neti, neti* – not this, not that!
Then drop *I and thou*
and say *neti, neti*.
What is left manifest in the emptiness –
that is truth,
and that alone is.
All else is dream.

114.

Love.
The decision to take *sannyas* is propitious –
and *sadhana* follows decision like a shadow.
Seeds have to be sown in the mind as well;
there too – as we sow we reap.
The way has to be carved out of the mind too.
The temple of God is close
but the mind is like a dense forest
we have to hack our way through to reach it.
The first steps have to be taken from where you are.
Even for a long journey
the first steps have to be taken just close by,
and in every journey,
not only that towards truth,
the beginning is not different from the end –
they are two ends of the same span,
two poles of the same entity.
Yet often you cannot guess from the first step
where you will end up;
those first steps may seem quite unrelated to the last!

Charles Catering recollects this interesting incident:
Once I bet a friend
that if I bought him a birdcage to hang in his sitting-room
he would have to buy a bird.
The friend laughed and said
he could keep a cage without a bird –

there was nothing to it!
He accepted the bet
and I bought him a beautiful cage from Switzerland
which he hung in his sitting-room.
Naturally, the inevitable happened –
life has its own logic.
Whosoever saw the cage
immediately sympathized with him,
asking:
When did your bird die?
He would answer: I never had a bird.
Then they would say: So why the empty cage?
Finally he got sick and tired of explaining
and went and bought a bird.
When I asked him about it he said:
It was easier to buy the bird and lose the bet
than to explain things to each and everyone
from morn till night.
And also,
seeing this empty cage hanging there
day in and day out, my mind kept repeating:
The bird! The bird! The bird!

So, if you hang commitment like a cage in the mind
it won't be long before the bird of _sadhana_ comes!

115.

Love.
Man lives not in reality but in dreams.
Each mind creates a world of its own
which exists nowhere.

During the day as well as the night
the mind is swamped in dreams.
When the dreams become too much, too intense,
insanity results.

To be clear and healthy is to be without dreams.

Once, the president of a country went to inspect
the nation's largest lunatic asylum.
The director took him to a room and told him:
In this room, the inmates suffer from car-phobia.
The president, curious, looked through the window.
But there is nobody there, he said.
They are all there, sir – under the beds repairing cars,
the director replied.

Everyone is lying under their dreams in the same way.
If this president had looked within,
what would he have found?
Is not every capital a great madhouse?
But one cannot see one's own madness –
this is a sure trait of madness.

When someone starts doubting himself,
seeing his madness,
know well that the time has come for his insanity to go.
Awareness of madness marks the end of madness.
Awareness of ignorance heralds its end.
Awareness of dreaming brings dreams to an end.
What is left is truth.

116.

Love.
I am very glad to have received your letter.
Anxieties exist in life
but there is no need to worry about them.
Worrying stems not from the anxieties but from our attitude
towards them.
To be anxious or not is always our open choice.

It is not that a non-anxious mind is free of anxieties – anxieties

are there, they are an unavoidable part of life –
but it does not burden itself with them.
Such a person always sees beyond them;
dark nights surround him too but his eyes look to the rising sun
and therefore his soul
is never drowned in darkness.
And this alone is enough –
that the soul not be drowned in darkness.
The body is bound to drown in it – in fact it already has.
Those who are condemned to die
live their lives in darkness;
only the deathless have their lives rooted in the light.

Blessings to the children and regards to all.

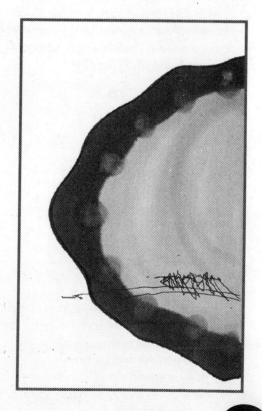

117.

Love.
There is no greater power than trusting oneself –
its fragrance is not of this world;
peace, bliss and truth flow from this fragrance.
He who trusts himself is in heaven
and he who mistrusts himself
holds the keys of hell in his hands.
The Scottish philosopher David Hume was an atheist,
but every Sunday he made it a point
to attend the sermon of John Brown, a confirmed theist.
When people pointed out
that going to church was against his own principles
he laughed – and replied: I have no faith whatever
in what John Brown says,
but John Brown has total faith in what John Brown says.
So once a week I make a point of hearing a man
who has total faith in himself!

118.

Love.
Love is also fire,
but a cool fire.
Yet we have to burn in it
because it also purifies;
it burns only to purify.
The dross burns
leaving pure gold.

In the same way my love will bring suffering
because I wish to destroy you in order to recreate you.
The seed must be broken –
how else can the tree be born?
The river must end –
how else is it to merge with the ocean?

So let go of yourself and die –
how else will you find the *self?*

119.

Love.
Truth is discovered not through swimming
but through drowning.
Swimming is a surface happening,
drowning takes you to the infinite depths.

120.

Love.
The search for meaning is disastrous;
it has brought nothing but meaninglessness.
To see that there is no meaning –
is to have the real meaning
where meaninglessness cannot be,
where meaning doesn't matter
and so its disasters are avoided.
What remains just is, and what is,
is and what is not, is not and that's all.

You ask for a clear statement about motivelessness.
Your attempt to understand cannot succeed
because it is motivated!

Why bother about understanding?
Look, isn't the thing clear before you there?
All things are open!
All things are clear!
But man is so busy understanding no one is left to see what is
clear, what is obvious, what is there!

Confusion is the effort to understand.

Ignorance is the effort to know.
If you don't try to understand or know,
nothing can hide itself from you!
Truth is always in front of you, naked, clear.

121.

Love.
You say you feel broken.
It would be better if you broke down completely
and disappeared.
That which is will always be the case
and that which has become is bound to vanish.
Becoming always leads to dissolution
so do not try to save yourself.
One who loses himself goes beyond life and death,
and he who saves himself is lost.
You are busy saving yourself
and that is why you are afraid of breaking down.
But what is there to save?
And that which is worth saving is already saved.

122.

Love.
You long for the sun
and you will get it for sure,
but you have to have the courage to burn!
You can't reach the light without dying,
for ego is darkness,
and besides, the sun isn't anywhere outside
but is born within when everything else there burns.
When the self is alight – that is the light.
The fear of dying is darkness,
the jump into death is the light.
Die, and know this!

Disappear, and you will find it.
That is why I say love is prayer –
it is the first lesson in death.

Regards to all.

123.

Love.
Do not look for a purpose in life but live, and live totally.
Do not be serious and grave but turn life into a dance.
Dance – like the waves on the sea!
Blossom – like the flowers in spring!
Sing – as the birds do continuously!
All without purpose, for no reason; then purpose is there,
and all mystery is solved.

The famous physician Rocky Tonsky once asked a student:
What is the purpose of life?
What is its meaning?
The student hesitated and stammered, as if trying to remember,
then said: Yesterday I knew, but right now
I seem to have forgotten.
Rocky Tonsky looked up at the sky and cried:
God in heaven!
The only man who ever knew and now he has forgotten!

Love to all the family.

124.

Love.
You ask for my ten *commandments*.
This is very difficult
because I am against any sort of commandment.
Yet just for the fun of it I set down what follows:

1. Obey no orders except those from within.
2. The only God is life itself.
3. Truth is within, do not look for it elsewhere.
4. Love is prayer.
5. Emptiness is the door to truth; it is the means,
    the end and the achievement.
6. Life is here and now.
7. Live *fully awake*.
8. Do not swim, float.
9. Die each moment
    so that you are renewed each moment.
10. Stop seeking. That which is, is: *stop and see*.

125.

Love.
The news of the commune delights me.
The tree's seed is sprouting,
soon innumerable souls will shelter under its branches.
Soon the people for whom I have come will gather –
and you are going to be their hostess!
So prepare yourself; that is, empty yourself completely
because only emptiness can be the host.
You are already on your way,
singing, dancing, blissful like a river flowing to the sea.
I am delighted, and I am always with you.
The ocean is close –
just run, run, run!

126.

Love.
Everything changes except change,
only change is eternal.
But the human mind lives in the past –
and that is the confusion of all confusions.

One day the sky was filled with the clouds of war –
plane upon plane loaded with death.
Beasts, birds, worms and beetles –
all that could flee, fled.
Horses, donkeys, rats, sheep, dogs and cats, wolves –
all ran for their lives
and the paths and tracks were full of them.
As they fled, this multitude saw
two vultures sitting on a wall by the road.
Brothers! they cried to them. Flee! At once!
Man is on the warpath again.
The vultures just smiled. They knew!
One said: Since time immemorial man's wars have been good
news for vultures.
Our ancestors have said so, and so too our scriptures.
It is also our own experience.
In fact it is for the benefit of vultures
that God sends man to war!
God has made man and war just for vultures!
This said, the two vultures flew off towards the battle –
and in the next moment were blown to pieces by falling bombs.

If they had only known how things
can change over thousands of years
But does even man himself realize this?

127.

Love.
I received your letter.
Don't be afraid of sexual desire
because fear is the beginning of defeat.
Accept it,
it is and it has to be.
Of course, you must know it and recognize it,
be aware of it,
bring it out of the unconscious into the conscious mind.

You cannot do this if you condemn it
because condemnation leads to repression
and it is repression that pushes desires and emotions
into the unconscious.

Really, it is because of repression
that the mind is divided into conscious and unconscious,
and this division is at the root of all conflict.
It is this division that prevents man from being total –
and without integration there is no way to peace,
bliss and freedom. So meditate on sexual desire.
Whenever the desire arises,
watch it mindfully.
Do not resist it,
do not escape from it.
Encountering it leads you to unique experiences.
And whatever you have learned
or heard about celibacy –
throw it once and for all into the dustbin,
for there is no way other than this
of reaching to brahmacharya.

My regards to all there.

128.

Love.
Be like steel – clay will no longer do.
To be a sannyasin is to be a soldier of God.
Serve your parents – even more than before.
Give them the joy of a sannyasin son.
But don't relent, keep your resolution firm;
it will bring glory to your family.
The son who compromises with a thing like sannyas
shames his family.
I have complete trust in you,
that's why I have been a witness to your sannyas.

Laugh and go through everything.
Listen to everything and laugh.
This is your _sadhana_.
Let the storms come and go.

129.

Love.
In _sannyas, samsara_ is just a drama;
to know the world as a play is _sannyas_.
Then no one is small,
no one great,
no Ram and no enemy, Ravan,
and everything is a _Ram-leela_, God's play.

Whichever part you are given play it well.
The part is not you
and as long as we identify with our part in the play
self-knowledge is impossible.
And from the day that this identification is broken
ignorance becomes impossible.

Play your part
but know well it isn't you.

130.

Love.
I have received your letter.
There is a great difference between love and pity.
There is pity in love
but there is no love in pity.
Therefore it is important to know things as they are:
love as love, pity as pity.
To take one for the other
is to create unnecessary worry.

Ordinarily, love has become impossible
because as he is man cannot be loving:
to be in love the mind must be completely empty
and we love only with our minds,
so that when our love is at its lowest it is sex
and at its highest it is compassion,
but love is a transcendence of both sex and compassion.

Therefore understand what is
and do not strive for what should be –
what should be flows out of
the acceptance and understanding of what is.

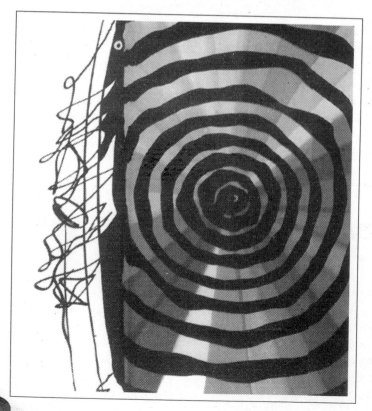

131.

Love.
I received your letter.
Now never worry about me,
not even mistakenly for two reasons.
First: the day I surrendered myself for God
I transcended all anxiety –
because trying to look after oneself
is the only anxiety!
Ego is anxiety.
Beyond it: what anxiety? whose? and for whom?
Secondly: men like me are born to be crucified.
The cross is our throne
and our mission is fulfilled
only when stones are showered, not flowers.

But on the divine path
even stones turn into flowers,
and on the contrary path
even flowers turn out to be stones.
Therefore when the stones start raining on me,
be happy and thank God!
Truth is always received like this.
If you don't agree
ask Socrates
ask Jesus
ask Buddha
ask Kabir
ask Meera.

My regards to all.

132.

Love.
What does the seed know of its own potential?
It is the same with man:
he doesn't know what he is nor what he can be!
The seed, perhaps, cannot look within but man can.
This looking in is called meditation.
To know one's truth
as it is here and now is meditation.
Dive into it, deeper and deeper;
there, in the depths, all that is possible
can be clearly seen.
And once seen it begins to happen –
the awareness of what is possible turns it into a reality,
like a seed stirred by a vision of its potential
beginning to sprout.
Time, effort, energy – pour it all into meditation
because meditation is the gateless gate through which
the self becomes aware of itself.

133.

Love.
Nothing in life is sure – except death,
otherwise life is another name for insecurity.
When this is realized
the desire for security simply vanishes.
To accept insecurity is to become free of it.
Uncertainty will stay in the mind
because that is its nature.
Don't worry about it
because that will add fuel to it.
Just let the mind be, where it is,
and you go into meditation.
You are not the mind
so where is the problem of the mind?

Leave the darkness where it is
and just light your lamp.
Are you going to think carefully and then surrender?

O mad one! Surrender is a leap outside thought.
Either jump or don't jump
but for God's sake don't ponder over it!

134.

Love.
Theism is another name for infinite hope.
It is patience,
it is waiting,
it is trust in *leela*,
in the play of life,
and therefore with theism complaining cannot be.
Theism is acceptance,
it is surrender –
acceptance of what is beyond the self
and surrender to the source of the self.

In 1914 a fire broke out in Thomas Edison's laboratory.
Machinery worth millions
and all the papers pertaining to his lifelong research
were burnt to ashes.
Hearing of this tragedy his son Charles
came looking for him
and he found him standing by the side
enjoying the sight of the leaping flames.
On seeing Charles, Edison said to him:
Where is your mother?
Go and find her and bring her here quickly;
such a sight she will never see again!

The next day, walking amidst the ashes
of his hopes and dreams,

the 67 year-old inventor said:
What benefit there is in destruction!
All our mistakes have been burnt to ashes, thank God!
Now we can begin afresh, all over again!

God's grace is endless.
We just need the eyes to see it.

135.

Love.
Wittgenstein has said somewhere:
Of that which one cannot speak,
one should remain silent.
Oh, if only this advice was heeded
there would be no useless arguments about truth!
That-which-is cannot be spoken of.
Whatever is said in words is not,
cannot be,
that-which-is.
Truth is beyond words,
only silence is related to truth.

But silence is very difficult;
the mind wants to speak even of that
which is beyond words.
Really, the mind is the only barrier to silence.
Silence belongs to the state of no-mind.

A preacher came to address some small children.
Before beginning he put a question to them:
If you were asked to address a gathering
of such intelligent boys and girls
who expect a good lecture from you,
and if you had nothing to speak on,
what would you say?
A small child replied: I would keep quiet.

I would keep quiet.
This child-like simplicity is needed to experiment with silence.

136.

Love.
Sannyas is a pilgrimage to Mt. Everest –
naturally there are difficulties on the way.
But the fruits of determination are sweet too,
so bear everything calmly and joyously
but don't give up your commitment.
Serve your mother even more than before –
sannyas is not a running away from responsibility.
Your family is not to be given up,
rather you have to make the whole world your family.
Encourage your mother to take *sannyas* too.
Tell her: You have seen enough of the world,
now raise your eyes towards God.
But make sure she is caused no trouble on your account.
This doesn't mean giving in or compromising –
sannyas knows no compromise.
Strong, bold and resolute is the soul of *sannyas*.

137.

Love.
Love does not discriminate
even in dreams,
and in that love which is prayer too,
there are no distinctions at all.

Now *I* am no more.
The word I is simply a convenience
and as such causes many difficulties.
When the clouds of the *I* disappear
nothing remains but love –

love without cause,
unconditional love.
Here I stand in the marketplace:
who is ready to come and take it from me?
Kabir stands in the marketplace, torch in hand.
If you are ready to burn your house down, come with me.

138.

Love.
Ah, if the veena were outside you could hear its music,
but it is inside
and we do not hear it.
But we can become one with it.
And how much is music worth that ends with listening?
Ultimately the musician, the veena, the music,
the listener
are not separate.
Look inside,
go within,
and see who is waiting there for you.

139.

Love.
The springs of meditation are close at hand
but the layers of suppressed sex work like rocks.
The repression of sex has choked your life with anger,
its smoke pervades your whole personality.
When you were meditating in front of me the other day
I saw all this very clearly,
but I could also see that your will is very strong too,
your thirst for God is also strong
and you are working hard,
so there is no need to be disheartened.
Difficulties are there,

blocks are there,
but they will disintegrate
because the breaker is not yet broken.

Meditate totally and soon the springs will be reached.
But you have to put your whole being at stake –
nothing less will do.
Hold back a bit and you will miss.
Time is short so gather all your strength;
whilst the opportunity is here
your effort must be total.

It is difficult to say whether you will have such an opportunity
in another life,
so everything must be finished in this one.
If the gates don't open this time
you will have to start from the very beginning next time –
and then it is far from sure that I will be with you.

In your last life you worked for it
but the work was not completed;
and it was the same in the life before that.
For three lives you have repeated the same cycle
again and again –
it is time now to break it.

It is already late,
any further delay would be foolish.
My regards to all.

140.

Love.
The meaning of *sadhana*
is to enter into one's own nature,
to live in it,
to be it.

One must therefore know what is not one's nature
so as to be aware what one wants to be free of.
Recognizing it becomes freedom from it.

A disciple of Bankei asked him:
I become overwhelmed by anger.
I want to be rid of it but I cannot be.
What shall I do?

Bankei did not say a word,
just stared deep into the eyes of the disciple,
who began to sweat
in those few heavy minutes of silence.

He wanted to break the silence
but couldn't gather the courage.
Then Bankei laughed and said: It's strange!
I searched and searched but could find
no anger within you.
Still, show me a little of it, here and now.

The disciple said: It is not always here.
It comes all of a sudden, how can I produce it now?

Bankei laughed again and said:
Then it is not your true nature.
That remains with you always,
and if your anger had been part of it
you could have shown it to me.
When you were born it was not with you,
when you die it will not be with you.
No, this anger is not you.
There is a mistake somewhere.
Go away and think again,
search again, meditate again.

141.

Love.
God purifies in every way.
It is not only gold that has to pass through fire
to be purified
but man too.
For man this fire is the anguish of love.

It is a blessing when this fire enters a person's life;
it is the fruit of infinite prayers, infinite births.
It is the intensity of thirst that turns finally into love,
but unfortunately few are able to welcome it
because few can recognize love in the form of anguish.

Love is not a throne, it is a cross;
but those who gladly offer
themselves to it attain the very highest throne.
The cross can be seen, the throne cannot –
it is always hidden behind the cross.
And even Jesus hesitated for a moment;
even his heart cried out: *Father, why hast thou forsaken me?*
But the next moment he remembered and said:
Thy will be done.

That was enough:
the cross became a throne
and death a new life.
In the moment of revolution
between one statement and the next
Christ descended into Jesus.

Your suffering is intense and a new birth is at hand;
be happy, be grateful.
Don't be afraid of death, be thankful.
It is the tidings of a new birth.
And the old must die to give birth to the new;
the seed must break to blossom into the flower.

142.

Love.
What is suppressed becomes attractive,
what is negated, beckons!
Only alertness to the mind's games brings freedom.
Negation does not really negate,
on the contrary, it beckons.
The mind plays around the forbidden
like the tongue around the gap of an extracted tooth.

A small shopkeeper in London once caused a sensation.
He hung in his show window
a black curtain with a small hole at the center;
under the hole was written in large letters:
Peeping strictly forbidden.
Naturally, it brought the traffic to a standstill!
Crowds gathered around the shop
jostling one another for a peep through the curtain.
There they saw nothing but a few towels –
it was just a small towel shop
and the shopkeeper had devised this sure-fire method
of increasing his sales.
It worked like magic.
Man's mind works the same way
and he becomes trapped by it.
Therefore – always be wary of negation,
opposition, suppression.

143.

Love and blessings.
Live the truth,
for there is no other way to find it.
Become the truth,
for there is no other way to know it.
You cannot know truth through words,

not through the scriptures,
nor through learning, study, contemplation.
Truth is within, in the emptiness within.
In the state of no-mind,
in the mind free of desires where only awareness is,
there truth manifests itself.
Truth simply is;
it has not to be found,
simply uncovered.
The lid of gold covering it is the ego.
Ego is darkness;
die, and become light!
Where the darkness of the ego is no more
there, in that emptiness, truth is;
and that is truth,
and that is bliss,
and that is immortality.
Do not seek it,
just die and it is there.

144.

Love.
I am glad to receive your letter.
Yes, this much suffering has to be gone through –
it is the birth pangs of our own rebirth.
And going back is not possible
for where is the past to which to return?
Time demolishes the steps we climb to reach the present.
There is no going back –
only going forward is possible,
forward and forward –
and the journey is endless!
There is no goal, no destination,
only resting places,
where the tents are dismantled
as soon as they are pitched.

But why this fear of anarchy?

All systems are false —
life is anarchic, insecure.
He who seeks security dies before his death.
Why this hurry to die?
Death itself will take care of that for us
so is it not right that we learn to live?

And the miracle is
that death does not call
on the one who learns how to live —
and this alone is needed.
Doesn't the gardener silently wait after sowing the seed?

Whenever you need me you will find me beside you.
Regards to all there.

145.

Love.
Atheism is the first step towards theism,
and a must.
If you haven't been through the fire of atheism
you'll never know the light of theism.
If you haven't the true strength to say No
your Yes will always be impotent.
So I am glad you are an atheist —
something that can be said only by a theist.

So I say: Go deeper into atheism.
Superficiality won't do,
so don't just think atheism, live it —
and it will ultimately lead you to God.
Atheism isn't it,
it is just a doubting.
Doubt is good but it isn't it.

Actually, doubt is a search for trust.
So go on, make your journey,
for the path to truth starts with this doubt.
Doubt is *sadhana*
because doubt eventually exposes the incontestable truth.

Inside the seed of doubt is the tree of trust,
so if you plant the seed of questioning
and work on it
you are bound to harvest trust.
And beware all religions!
Only religions obstruct the true path of *religion*.

146.

Love.
Dreams too are true
because what we call truth is only a dream –
it is just the difference between open and closed eyes.
Understand this fully
and then one can go beyond both,
and the way lies beyond both.
Both are *the seen* and beyond both is the seer.

147.

Love.
Not only is a seed a seed,
man is also a seed.
Not only seeds bloom,
man also blooms.
Not only seeds blossom into flowers.

148.

Love.
How can the search begin unless there is doubt?
How will the heart awaken to know the truth
unless there is doubt?
Remember – belief and faith bind man,
doubt liberates him.

149.

Love.
I was glad to receive your letter.
Make love your prayer now.
Love alone is worship, is God.
Let there be love with every breath –
this is your only *sadhana*.
Sitting, rising, sleeping, waking
just remember: *love*.
Then you will see that his temple is not far off.

150.

Love.
God is testing you every moment.
Laugh and take the test –
it is beautiful that he considers you worth testing!
But don't be in a hurry
for the more you hurry the more some goals recede,
and without doubt the temple of God is a goal like that.
He who travels with patience travels fastest on this journey.
The mind will roam again and again –
that is its way;
the day its roaming stops it will be dead.
Sometimes it sleeps –
do not mistake this for death.

Sometimes it gets tired –
don't mistake this for death either.
Some rest and sleep and it is strong and alive again.
So stop bothering about it altogether
for even this worry gives it strength.
Surrender even this to God.
Say to him: Whatever it's like, good or bad,
take care of it .
And then just be a witness,
simply watch the whole play.
Watch the play of the mind with detachment
and then suddenly –
there is the consciousness which is no-mind.

151.

Love.
God is far off because we don't know
how to see him close by.
Actually there is nothing closer than him.
More than that – he is the here and now.
The name God is just for those
who can't find the here and now.
Words, names, doctrines, scriptures, religion, philosophy,
all these are created for those who can see him
only at a distance.
Hence they have no connection with God
but only with those who are blind to the near.
That's why I say: Drop the distant.
Drop paradises in the sky.
Drop hopes in the future,
and see the near in time and in space.
Be here and now and see!
See the instant in time,
see the atom in space.
In the _time moment_ time ceases to exist.
In the _space atom_ space ceases to exist.

There is no space, no time, here and now.

What is left is truth,
is God,
is *that*.
You too are that.
Tat twam asi – that art thou.

152.

Love.
Religion too has to take new birth in every age.
Bodies – all kinds of bodies – grow old and die.
Sects are the dead bodies of religion,
their souls have left them long ago.
Their languages have become out of date.
This is why they no longer touch
the human heart any more.
Nor is their echo heard any more in the human soul.

Once Dr. John A. Hutton, while speaking in a gathering of priests
asked, "Why have the preachings of religious leaders turned so
lifeless and dull?"

When nobody stood up to answer,
he himself answered it by saying:
"They are all dull because preachers are trying to answer questions that nobody is asking."

Religiousness is eternal.
But its body should always be contemporary.
Neither is the body eternal, nor can it be –
not even the body of religion.

153.

Love.
Drop the fear,
because the moment you hold on to it, it multiplies.
To hold on to it is to nourish it.
But dropping fear does not mean fighting with it.
To fight is also to hold on to it.
Just know that fear is.
Do not run away from it,
do not escape.
In life there is fear,
there is insecurity,
there is death –
just know this.
All these are facts of life.
Where would you run from them?
How would you avoid them?
Life itself is such.
And its acceptance, its natural acceptance,
is the freedom from fear.
Once fear is accepted, where is it?
Once death is accepted, where is it?
Once insecurity is accepted, where is it?
Acceptance of the wholeness of life is what I call
sannyas, initiation on the path.

154.

Love.
Attainment of meditation is not a question of time,
it is a question of will.
If the will is total, meditation happens in a moment too.
And a mind without will can go on wandering
for lives upon lives.
Intensify the will.
Crystallize the will.

Make the will total.
And then, meditation will knock
upon your door on its own.
And the mind certainly tortures one as long as meditation is
absent.
Mind is the name for the absence of meditation,
just as darkness is the name for the absence of light.
As the light arrives, darkness leaves.
As meditation arrives, the mind leaves.
Hence, now drown into meditation.
All else follows on its own.

155.

Love.
The world is neither unhappiness nor happiness.
The world becomes the same as we see it.
Our vision is the world.
Each person is the creator of his own world.
If every moment of life gives you unhappiness, then the mistake
is somewhere in your own vision.
And if all that you see around you is darkness, then certainly you
are keeping closed the eyes that see light.
Give a fresh thought to yourself.
Look at yourself from a new angle.
If you put the blame on others, you will never be able to see
your own mistake.
If you put the blame on circumstances, you will not be able to
penetrate the roots of your own mental state.
Hence, whatever the situation, proceed to discover its causes in
yourself.
Causes are always in one's own self.
But they always appear to be in others.
Avoid this mistake and it will be difficult
to preserve your unhappiness.
Others function only as mirrors.
The face seen is always our own.

Life can become a celebration.
But it is necessary to create oneself anew.
And that is not a difficult thing.
Because in the very seeing of the fault in one's own vision the
mistakes start dying
and the birth of a new person begins.

156.

Love.
Do not fight with yourself.
Such a fight is futile.
Because victory never, ever comes through it.
To fight with oneself
is nothing other than a gradual suicide.
Accept yourself.
Happily. In gratitude.
What is, is good.
Sex too, anger too.
Because whatsoever is, is from the divine.
Accept it and understand it.
Search and uncover the hidden potential in it.
Then, even sex feels to be a seed towards the divine.
And anger becomes the door to forgiveness.
Evil is not an enemy of goodness.
Rather, evil is only imprisoned goodness.

157.

Love.
Strive for meditation.
Then all problems of the mind will disappear.
In fact, mind is the problem.
All the rest of the problems are only echoes of the mind.
Nothing will come of fighting
each and every problem separately.

Fighting with echoes is futile,
there is no outcome of it other than defeat.
Do not prune the branches,
because four other branches
will replace that one pruned branch.
By pruning branches, the tree only grows more.
And, the problems are the branches.
If you want to cut at all, cut the roots,
because by cutting the roots
the branches disappear on their own.
And mind is the root.
Cut this root with meditation.
Mind is the problem.
Meditation is the solution.
Mind knows no solution.
Meditation knows no problem.
Because, there is no meditation in the mind.
Because, there is no mind in meditation.
Absence of meditation is mind.
Disappearance of mind is meditation.
This is why I say: strive for meditation.

158.

Love.
Don't be in haste.
Maintain patience.
Patience is a fertilizer for meditation.
Go on tending meditation,
the fruit is bound to come,
it always comes.
But, do not be anxious about the fruit.
Because such an anxiety itself
becomes an obstacle for the fruit.
Because such a worry distracts the attention
from meditation.
Meditation requires total attention.

To be divided won't do.
Partiality won't do.
Meditation is not possible without your totality.
Hence, stay with the act of meditation and leave the fruit of
meditation in the hands of the divine.
And the fruit comes.
Because drowning totally in meditation
is the birth of the fruit.

159.

Love.
Life is not divided, either in time or in space.
If life is anything, it is undividedness –
it is an undivided flow.
Past, present, future – these are human lines drawn on the undi-
vided flow of time.
Indeed, they are nowhere except in the minds of men.
Mind is time.
Similarly, space is also undivided.
The body is not one's limit –
in fact, the limit or non-limit of the whole is one's limit.
But, the mind does not rest without dividing.
It is like a prism; to divide is its function.
Passing through it the ray of existence becomes divided into
many rays and many colors.
What is one at the root becomes many at the branches.
The root is eternal – beginningless, endless.
Branches are in time –
they have their beginning, they have their end.
Branches are change.
The root is ever-lasting.
Neither the root changes nor can it be changed.
Yes – one can desire it to be changed, and then such a desire
inevitably takes one into failure and anguish.
Branches go on changing.
They cannot be stopped from changing.

But certainly it can be desired that they don't change, and then
such a desire inevitably
transforms itself into failure and anguish.
The West is in the first kind of failure and anguish.
The East is in the second kind of failure and anguish.
And so far man has not been able to give birth to such a culture
which not only succeeds but becomes fulfilled too.
The two realities I have talked about above –
the reality of the root and the reality of the branches;
the law of the intransient and the law of the transient –
it is only in the harmonious balance of these two that
such a culture can be born which will neither be polar
nor lopsided, which will use the tension of the opposite poles,
the same as architecture uses opposing bricks in creation of
an arched door.
The truth of life is pluralism.
And, the stream of life always flows taking the opposite poles
as its banks.

160.

Love.
We just do not know life, that is why we get bored.
We make life mechanical, that is why we get bored.
We are not living life, we only drag along with it,
that is why we get bored.
Boredom is not in life,
rather it comes out of our fear of living.
We are not only afraid of death –
we are afraid of life as well.
In fact, we fear death because we fear life.
Otherwise, death is not the end of life –
it is the completion of life.
This is why I say: live – live fearlessly.
Let go of the past:
man goes on carrying it because of fear.
And do not invite dreams of the future,

because in order to avoid living today
man plans for living in the future.
Live today, and now, and here.
'Tomorrow' is a deception –
the 'tomorrow' that has passed as yesterday,
as well as the tomorrow that is yet to come.
Only this moment is.
Only this moment is eternal.

161.

Love.
Life is a mystery.
It can be lived.
It can also be known by living it.
But it cannot be solved like a mathematical problem.
It is not a problem – it is a challenge.
It is not a question – it is an adventure.
Hence, those who only go on asking questions about life remain,
by this action, deprived of the answer forever.
Or acquire answers which are not answers at all.
It is such answers that one acquires from scriptures.
In fact, an answer acquired from any other source
cannot be an answer.
Because the truth of life cannot be borrowed.
Or such questioners fabricate answers of their own;
thus they certainly gain consolation, but not solutions.
Because fabricated answers are not answers.
Only the experience can be an answer.
Hence, I say: do not ask – live and know.
This is the difference between philosophy and religion.
To ask is philosophy, to live is religiousness.
And, the interesting thing is that philosophy asks
but never gets the answer, and religion does not ask at all
and yet attains the answer.

162.

Love.
Society is only a collectivity of individuals.
Hence, finally and essentially,
it is a reflection of the minds of the individuals.
If the individual mind is without peace,
the society cannot be at peace.
Only a radical transformation of the individual mind
can become the peace of the society.
There is no other alternative.
Nor is there any shortcut.
The technique for individual transformation is meditation.
With more and more people moving into meditation; only then
is something possible.
To take shelter in the divine is the only way.

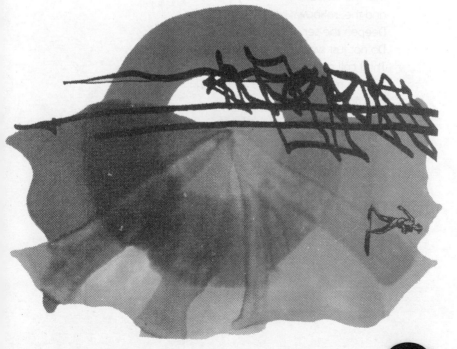

1971

163.

Love.
You ask for the way to make the invisible visible?
Pay attention to the visible.
Do not just see, pay attention.
It means, when you see a flower,
let your whole being become the eye.
When you listen to the birds,
let your entire body-soul become the ear.
When you look at a flower, do not think.
When you listen to birds, do not ponder.
Let the total consciousness
either see or hear or smell or taste or touch.
Because it is due to a shallowness of sensitivity
that the invisible is unable to become visible,
and the unknown remains unknown.
Deepen the sensitivity.
Do not just swim in sensitivity, drown in it.
This I call meditation.
And, in meditation, the seen disappears
and finally the seer too.
There remains only the seeing.
It is in this seeing that the invisible becomes visible
and the unknown becomes known.
Not only this – even the unknowable becomes knowable.
And remember that whatever I am writing –
do not start thinking about this as well: act.
Nothing has ever been nor can be attained
by creating theories.
There is no other door except 'seeing for oneself'.

164.

Love.
You ask: how far is the destination?
Ah! The destination is very far, and very near too.
And the distance or the nearness of the destination
is not dependent on the destination but upon you yourself.
The deeper the will, the nearer the destination.
If the will is total, then you yourself are the destination.

165.

Love.
The word is not the thing –
the word *God* is not God.
But the mind goes on accumulating words and
words and words,
and then the words become the barrier.

See this as a fact with you:
can you see anything without the word?
Can you feel anything without the word?
Can you live even for a single moment without the word?
Do not think but *see*.
and then you will be in meditation.

To exist wordlessly is to be in meditation.

166.

Love.
Always see *what is* –
the facts.
That which is.
Do not project anything,
do not interpret,

do not impose any meaning:
that is, do not allow your mind to interfere,
and you will begin to encounter reality.
Otherwise everyone lives in his own world of dreaming.
And meditation is the coming out of these worlds,
these dreaming patterns.

A philosopher stopped Mulla Nasrudin on the street.
In order to test whether the Mulla
was sensitive to philosophical knowledge
he made a sign, pointing at the sky.
The philosopher meant: There is only one truth, which covers all.
Nasrudin's companion, an ordinary man, thought:
The philosopher is mad.
I wonder what precautions Nasrudin will take.
Nasrudin looked in his knapsack and took out a coil of rope.
This he handed to his companion.

Excellent, thought the companion.
We will bind him up if he becomes violent.

The philosopher saw that Nasrudin meant:
Ordinary humanity tries to find truth by methods
as unsuitable as attempting to climb into the sky with a rope.

Now can you remain content with the fact
of Mulla Nasrudin giving the rope to his companion
without any interpretation whatsoever?

Remain with the fact, and you will be in meditation.

167.

Love.
The ego is necessary
for both the sensation of pain and the feeling of pleasure
and vice versa also —

the sensation of pain and the feeling of pleasure,
are necessary for the existence of the ego.
In fact these are two sides of the same coin.
The name of the coin is *ignorance*.

Understand this
and do not fight with the ego
or with pain and pleasure,
because unless ignorance is gone
they will not go, they cannot go.
And you cannot fight with ignorance
because ignorance is just absence of something –
absence of yourself.
So be present to your ignorance,
be aware of it,
and then you will be and there will be no ignorance
because you and ignorance cannot exist simultaneously,
as with light and darkness.

168.

Love.
A small boy with a penny
clutched tightly in his hot little hand
entered the toyshop
and drove the proprietor to distraction
asking him to show this and that
and everything
without ever making up his mind.

Look here, my boy, said the storekeeper finally.
What do you want to buy for a penny –
the whole world with a fence around it?

The boy thought for a moment
and then replied: Let me see it.
And I say to you that ordinarily

no one in this world is different from that small boy.
But unless one is different, one is not mature.
And maturity does not come with age alone,
maturity comes through understanding the distinction
between that which is possible
and that which is not possible.

169.

Love.
Things go on changing without.
You must mirror them,
you must reflect them,
but remember always that the mirror remains the same.
Mirroring does not change the mirror.
Do not be identified with mirroring.
Remember yourself as the mirror –
that is what is meant by *witnessing*.
And witnessing is meditation.

Lieh-Tzu exhibited his skill in archery to Po-Hun Wu-Jen.
When the bow was drawn to its full length
a cup of water was placed on his elbow
and he began to shoot.
As soon as the first arrow was let fly
a second one was already on the string
and a third followed.
In the meantime he stood unmoved like a statue.
Po-Hun Wu-Jen said: The technique of your shooting is fine,
but it is still a technique.
You look just like a statue from without.
Now let us go up to a high mountain
and stand on a rock projecting over a precipice
and then you try to shoot.

They climbed up a mountain.
Standing on a rock projecting over a precipice

ten thousand feet high
Po-Hun Wu-Jen stepped backward
until one third of his feet was hanging over the rock.
He then motioned to Lieh-Tzu to come forward.
Lieh-Tzu fell to the ground
with perspiration running down to his heels.

Po-Hun Wu-Jen said:
The perfect man soars up above the blue sky
or dives down to the yellow springs,
or wanders about all over the eight limits of the world,
yet shows no signs of change in his spirit.
But you betray a sign of trepidation
and your eyes are dazed.
How can you expect to hit the target?

170.

Love.
Do you want to ask questions?
Or do you want to get answers?
Because if you want to ask questions
then you will not get answers,
and if you want to get answers
then you cannot be allowed to ask questions –
because the answer is in that consciousness
where the questions have not yet been raised,
or have been uprooted and thrown out.

171.

Love.
I hope you will be moving in deep meditation.
Breathe in it
sleep in it
live in it –

let meditation be your very existence.
Only then is *the happening*.
Don't do it, but be it.
And my blessings are always with you.
If you need any help from me just ask when
you are thoughtless,
and it will be given to you.

172.

Love.
A madman entered the bazaar and declaimed:
The moon is more useful than the sun.
But why? asked someone.
We need the light more
during the night than during the day, he said.
And I say to you that
all our metaphysical theories and explanations
are not of more worth than the explanation of that madman.

173.

Love.
Ask for nothing and you will never be frustrated.
Anticipate darkness with light and sorrow with happiness
because such is the nature of things.
Then you will never be frustrated.
Say to life: What can you do to me? I want nothing!
And say to death: What can you do to me?
I have already died!
Then you will be truly free,
because unless one is free of life
one can never be free of death.
And when one is free of both
one knows that life which is eternity itself.

174.

Love.
Man is always lacking,
because he desires without knowing himself,
because he desires to *become* something
without knowing his *being*,
and this is absurd.

First one must know his being
otherwise there will be anguish.

Becoming is anguish
because it is a constant tension
between that which is and that which should be –
and it is an impossible longing also
because only *that* can be which is.

So know yourself as you are
without any ideals,
without any judgment
and without any condemnation.
Go deep within yourself without any desires to become
because only then can you know yourself.

Discover yourself,
not according to anybody else,
but as you are.
Discover the fact,
discover the real
in its total nakedness.

In this total authenticity
just be a witness,
and then there is an altogether different quality to life,
the quality of *let go.*
Then one is relaxed totally.

And all flowering is in relaxation,
and all benediction.

175.

Love.
Fear cripples consciousness,
and fear is the source of unconsciousness,
that is why
without transcending fear
no one can attain to full consciousness.

But what is fear?
Fear is awareness of death
without knowing what death is.
Fear exists in the gap between you and your death,
and if there is no gap, no space,
then there is no fear.

Do not think of death as something outside you
because it is not.
And do not think of death as something in the future
because it is not.

Death is within you,
because death is the other side of life.
Life cannot exist without death;
they both belong to the same energy as positive and negative
poles.

So do not identify yourself with life —
because you are both.
The identification with life creates the gap.
And death has nothing to do with the future,
it is always here and now.
Every moment, it is.
And when one ceases to regard it

as something outside oneself
and, so to speak, draws it into his consciousness
and assimilates the idea of it,
one is completely changed.
He is in all truth born again.
And then there is no fear
because then there is no gap.

176.

Love.
Thinking is necessary but not enough,
one must know *living* also,
otherwise one becomes like the philosopher
mentioned by Soren Kierkegaard
who builds a fine palace
but is doomed not to live in it.
He has a shed for himself next door to what
he has constructed for others,
including himself, to look at!
Meditation is not thinking, but living.
Live it daily, moment to moment;
that is, live in it or let it live in you.
It is not something other-worldly either,
because all such distinctions are from the mind:
they are speculative and not existential,
and meditation is existential.
It is no more than one's everyday life *lived* totally.

When Mencius says: The truth is near
and people seek it far away,
he means *this*.
When Tokusan is asked about it he replies:

When you are hungry you eat,
when you are thirsty you drink,
and when you meet a friend you greet him.

He means *this*.
Ho Koji sings: How wondrous this, how mysterious!
I carry fuel, I draw water.
He also means *this*.
And when you are near me
whatsoever I may say I always mean *this*.
Or I may not say anything –
but then too I always mean *this*.

177.

Love.
Religion is so much an experience
that it cannot be handed over by one to another.
But there are traditions of religious experience –
which are bound to be false
because of the very nature of the religious experience.
One has to travel the path alone
with no footprints of other travellers even to guide one.

Hasan of Basra was asked: What is Islam and who
are the Muslims?
He is reported to have said:
Islam is in the books
and Muslims? Muslims are in the tombs.

178.

Love.
The world itself is a punishment enough,
so really there is no need for hell at all.

Once a man who had three wives
was brought before the king
of the country for punishment.
The king called in his counselors

and asked them to devise
the worst possible punishment for the offender,
even death itself.
But they did not order his execution,
ruling instead that it would be still worse for him
to live with all three wives at the same time.
Two weeks later the man committed suicide.

179.

Love.
I have no special doctrine or philosophy,
no set of concepts or intellectual formulas,
but only certain irrational devices
through which I can push you into the unknown.

I do not believe in any theories
or any systems of thought,
but I have faith in certain existential situations
through which I can throw you into the unknown.

Intellectual understanding is not understanding at all
but only a deception.
Understanding is always of the total,
of the whole being.
Intellect is only a part, and that too a minor one,
but it acts as the whole
and thereby creates all sorts of stupidities.

Do not be identified with your intellect.
Dissolve it into the whole of your being,
and then you will know what understanding is –
and the bliss and the ecstasy that follow it inevitably.

180.

Love.
Meditation is a mirror –
and the most faithful one.
Whoever goes into meditation
risks a confrontation with himself.
The mirror of meditation never lies,
and it does not flatter.
It is impartial and innocent
and it never projects anything.
It only faithfully shows your real, original face,
the face we never show to the world,
the face that we ourselves have forgotten.
So it is possible
that you yourself
may not be able to recognize it the first time!

But do not escape from it.
Face it and you will come to know it and recognize it.

This confrontation is the first test of courage
on the inner way.
So when it comes about –
rejoice and feel blessed.

181.

Love.
Yes, there is tension.
To be consciously conscious is to be tense,
but it is not because of consciousness
but because of *partial* consciousness.
The unconscious is always
behind the so-called consciousness.
This situation creates tension
because this creates a dichotomy, a duality;

hence the tension.
The being, which cannot be divided,
is divided,
hence the tension.

The unnaturalness of the situation
is the root cause of this tension,
and for that matter of all tensions,
because then one is not individual,
that is, indivisible;
therefore there is tension,
and one cannot really relax unless one is one.

Either be totally unconscious as in deep and
dreamless sleep –
and then there is no tension,
or be totally conscious –
and then you are in the state of no-tension
because the total can never be tense.
That is why the whole is the holy.

But falling into a deep sleep-like trance
is just escaping the problem,
and that too only for the time being,
because you will be back soon –
and worse off,
because by such escapes
the gap between
the conscious and the unconscious
is not bridged
but, on the contrary, widened even more.
One becomes split and schizophrenic.

So always be aware of the mind
because it tries to find solace in unconscious states
in so many ways –
through chemical drugs,
through auto-hypnotic means, and otherwise.

Begin to be aware of anything
which ordinarily happens unconsciously,
for example – anger, jealousy, pride –
and your consciousness will be deepened.

Act consciously,
even in day-to-day acts be conscious,
for example walking, eating, talking,
and your consciousness will be expanded.

Be alert when thinking.
No thought should be allowed to pass unwitnessed.

And then, in the end, there is an explosion
in which you become totally conscious,
with no unconsciousness behind.
When this happens one is *one*,
and to be one is to be silent.
This silence is beyond time and space,
because it is beyond duality.

182.

Love.
God is when you are not.
When you are it is not
because *you* are nothing but a blindness.
The ego cannot see,
the ego cannot be aware,
the ego exists only as a by-product of unconscious living.
One goes on living as if in sleep.
In this sleep the part begins to dream that it is *the whole*,
and this dreaming becomes a barrier to knowing *the whole*.

Begin to be aware,
aware of your actions, thoughts and emotions,
just *aware*.

Because if you condemn or appreciate
you will not be aware –
in any choice the awareness is contaminated
and the darkness of unawareness comes in.
So just be aware without any choice;
then awareness is pure and innocent,
and then awareness is a mirror.
In this mirror-like awareness one never finds oneself
but one finds *that-which-is*.
And that is God.

But it is only when you are not
because you are the dust which makes the mirror blind.
Because you are the blindness.

183.

Love.
There are three forms of knowledge.
The first is intellectual knowledge,
which is in fact not knowledge but only information
and the collection of facts and the use of these
to arrive at further intellectual concepts.
The second is emotional knowledge,
which is also not really knowledge
but the mental state in which man feels
he has known something,
but there is no transformation or mutation of his being.

The first is objective, and out of it science is born,
and the second is subjective, and is the source of all art.
The third is neither,
it is beyond both,
and this third is the real.
It is achieved through meditation
because meditation does not use thinking and feeling
as doors of perception.

Really, these are not doors of perception
but forces of projection.
Through them pure knowing is impossible;
whatsoever comes through them
is changed and colored by them.
So unless one is free of all projections
one cannot know *that-which-is*.
When there are no ripples of thought and emotion
in the consciousness, then and only then
does the third form of knowledge dawn,
and this third is the only real knowledge.
Out of it religion is born,
and out of it is total transformation.

184.

Love.
The journey is long
and the path is pathless.
And one has to be alone –
there is no map and no guide.

But there is no alternative.
One cannot escape it,
one cannot evade it.
One has to go on the journey.

The goal seems impossible
but the urge to go on it is intrinsic.
The need is deep in the soul.

Really, you are the urge, you are the need –
and consciousness cannot be otherwise
because of this challenge
and because of this adventure.
So do not waste time – *begin.*
Do not calculate – *begin.*

Do not hesitate – *begin*.
Do not look back – *begin*.

And always remember old Lao Tzu's words:
A tree that takes both arms to be encircled
grows from a tiny root.
A many-storied pagoda
is built by placing one brick upon another brick.
A journey of three thousand miles is begun
by a single step.

185.

Love.
When I say mutation I do not mean simply change.
Change is from the known to the known.
A sinner becomes a saint –
then it is change and not mutation.
You can practice change
but you cannot practice mutation
because only the known can be practiced –
and then any change is going to be only a modified past
because the past will be continuous in it,
and the past also will be the master of it
because it is cultivated by the past.

In other words, change is from *this* to that,
it is a movement in the known.
But mutation is an explosion:
from *this* to nothingness,
from here to nowhere.
You cannot practice it –
on the contrary, *you are the only hindrance*.

So what is to be done?
Really nothing can be done.
Be aware of this helplessness,

and remain in this helplessness.
Do not do anything
because any doing will be escaping
from this fact of helplessness.
Do not move at all –
and then there is an explosion,
and then there is mutation.

186.

Love.
Religion is not a promise for the future
but an experience *here and now*.
But through the priesthood it has become
promises and promises and promises.

At an examination of a class in First Aid
a member, who was also a priest, was asked:
What would you do if you found a man in a fainting condition?
I would give him some brandy, was the answer.
And if there was no brandy? he was then asked.
I would promise him some, replied the priest.

187.

Love.
Wherever there are words there is no real meaning.

But here also are words.
Then what to do?
Read between the words.
Or read that which is *said* but not written,
or that which is *shown* and not even said,
or that which is *meant* and not even shown.

That is – *look in,*

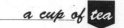

·because the words are without
but the meaning is within.

188.

Love.
Reason is not enough;
it is·necessary but not enough.
The *beyond must* be remembered – and always,
because reason in itself is destructive;
alone, it is nothing but an implement to dissect.
It makes a man anti-all and pro-nothing.
It creates absolutely negative minds
which can criticize but cannot create,
because reason has no healing force within itself.
It is only a tiny part and not the whole of life,
and the healing force is always with the *whole*.

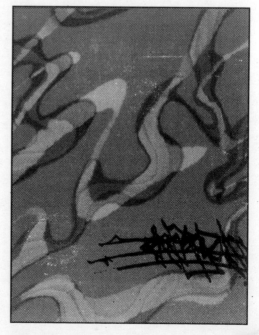

189.

Love.
With thought the mind has boundaries
but without thought the mind is just infinite space.

That is why in thoughtless awareness
one stops being a drop
and becomes oceanic.
And then there is great energy.
This energy wipes out everything which is dead.
It wipes out the whole karmic past –
and with no effort at all.
The greater absorbs the lesser and remains untouched.

190.

Love.
The will to wholeness is inherent in everything,
but only in man has it become conscious.
Therefore man lives in tension,
and only when this longing is fulfilled
is his negative state of tension erased.
The tension is symbolic of the infinite potential
and also of the infinite possibilities. ·

Man is not what he can be,
and unless he is that which he can be
he cannot be at ease.
This dis-ease is man,
and health is in wholeness.

The fact that language has one root
for the words *whole, holy* and to *heal*
conceals a deep truth:
He who is whole is also healed,
and to be healed is to be whole.

This wholeness can only be achieved
by becoming totally conscious of oneself:
The darkness of the unconscious is to be penetrated
and transformed into light.

And meditation is the method.

191.

Love.
The new world revealed in meditation
is not something added from the outside.
It has always been there – within,
is in *being* itself.
It *is* being itself.

One may know it or not, but it is *there* –
as a seed, of course, as a potentiality.
One has to make it actual, that is all.
That is why when it is revealed,
when it flowers,
one laughs uproariously
because it has always been there and one never knew it.

To work towards meditation is just like sculpturing
because as the sculptor chisels out a figure
deeply buried in a mass of inert matter,
so the meditator transforms his own inert potentialities
into living, dynamic and conscious creations.

Of course, here
the creator and the creation
and the means of creation
are not different but one
because the meditator himself is all.

And that is why I call meditation the greatest art.

192.

Love.
Do not think of others and waste your time;
really, that is a subtle and cunning way of the mind
to escape from itself.

Once a monk asked Ummon:
Sir, you always say that Buddhism helps us in
every possible way,
but how can it help the blind, the deaf or the dumb?
The blind cannot see the teacher's staff
that is raised before them,
the deaf cannot hear the teacher's words,
no matter how wise,
the dumb cannot ask their questions or speak
their understanding:
so since we cannot help these people
how can we say that Buddhism helps in every possible way?
What good is it?
Ummon just remained silent for a while
and then abruptly poked at the questioner with his stick.
The monk of course jumped back.
Ah! said Ummon. I see you are not blind!
Then he told the monk to come forward, which he did.
Ah-ha! said Ummon. I see you are not deaf!
Then he asked the monk
if he understood what all this to-do was about.
The monk said he did not.
Ah-ha! said Ummon. I see you are not dumb!

193.

Love.
Meditation does not require any application of the mind
or use of effort.
It descends upon you as effortlessly as sleep.

You cannot *try* to sleep,
nor can you *try* to meditate.
On the contrary,
every effort hinders its smooth and silent coming.

There is no place in it for action or aggression –
and action is always aggressive.
Meditation is passive receptivity.

Mind is aggressive,
meditation is passive.
Be passive
and receptive
and open
and vulnerable
and *wait.*
The real miracle happens through waiting.
The moment that waiting is total
there is a *happening,*
and – the explosion.

194.

Love.
The problem of life is not philosophical,
it is existential.
You cannot solve it from the outside;
you cannot just be a spectator of it –
you are in it, you *are it.*

And moreover, what is philosophy?
At the worst a linguistic misunderstanding,
or at best a linguistic analysis.
And even at its best it leads nowhere
because the problem is existential
and it cannot be solved through
language analysis and grammar.

One dark night a dervish was passing a dry well
when he heard a cry for help from below.
What is the matter? he called down.
I am a grammarian,
and I have unfortunately fallen,
due to my ignorance of the path, into this deep well,
in which I am now all but immobilized,
responded the other.
Hold on, friend, and I'll fetch a ladder and a rope,
said the dervish.
One moment please! said the grammarian.
Your grammar and diction are faulty.
Be good enough to amend them.
If that is so much more important than the essentials,
shouted the dervish, you had best stay where you are
until I have learned to speak properly.
And he went his way.

195.

Love.
Don't think about surrender at all
because *that which thinks about it is the only barrier.*
And therefore no one can surrender;
it is not a doing at all, it happens.
You cannot go to it,
it comes to you.
And any effort on your part will hinder its coming.
Be open and effortless, relaxed and passive,
and it will come – it always comes.
I am a witness of it.

196.

Love.
Mulla Nasrudin was searching for something on the ground.

What have you lost, Mulla?
someone who saw him searching, asked.
My key, said the Mulla.
So they both went down on their knees and looked for it.
After a time the other man asked:
Where exactly did you drop it?
In my house, said the Mulla.

Then why are you looking here?

There is more light here than inside my house.

I ask you also – where are you looking for the key?
Inside the house?
Or out there, where there is more light?

197.

Love.
There is no end to man's self-deception, because whatsoever he
is going to do he can rationalize it.

One day one man boasted in the bar
that he was a man of iron *will*,
and now he would prove it
by not touching wine again in his life.
But not even that day could pass by.
In the evening he came to the bar
and said loudly for all to hear –
I am stronger than my willpower.
I fought the whole day and finally conquered
my damn willpower!
A double scotch, please!

198.

Love.
The way of meditation is above the self;
its base is surrendering.
Surrender the self to your own no-self;
Be as if you are not.
Oh, the benediction
when one just leaves everything to the no-self!

Buddha called this phenomenon *anatma* or *anatta*
(no-selfhood).

One must turn oneself into a puppet
in the hands of the no-self,
and then everything begins to flow naturally
and spontaneously
just like a river flowing to the sea
or like a cloud wandering in the sky.

Lao Tzu says this is *doing by non-doing.*

One ceases to be one's own master
and becomes an instrument of the unknown –
and what nonsense it is to be one's own master
because there is no one to be so!

Do not search and you will continue to believe in it.
Search and it is nowhere to be found.

The self exists only in ignorance.
It is ignorance.
In *knowing* there is no self
because there is no knower.

Then knowing is enough unto itself.

199.

Love.
There is conflict in the mind – always,
because the mind cannot exist without the conflict.
It gets strengthened through conflict;
even warring against conflict is conflict
and struggling to go beyond the mind is mind.

See this deeply
and immediately
without motive,
just as if you have come across a snake in the street
 – and the jump.
Then it is not that you jump
but – *the jump.*
The jump happens spontaneously,
without effort and without conflict.
When this happens there is no-mind
and no-mind is the door to the divine.

200.

Love.
In meditation, enjoy doing nothing.
Be in a state of perfectly quiet passivity –
then you are in harmony with the world.
The thought-forms dissolve automatically
because they cannot exist with total passivity:
they are forms of an activity-addicted mind,
and with them dissolves the ego –
because it cannot exist without thought-forms.
The ego is nothing but a whirlpool center
of constantly revolving thought-forms.

Remain in passivity,
that is, in the state of absolute doing-nothingness,
and meditation deepens to the depths
where there is no meditator.
And remember that only when there is no meditator
has meditation really come into being.
If *you are* then there is no meditation,
and when there is meditation *you are not.*

201.

Love.
It is tragic but true that few people ever
possess their souls.
They possess everything except themselves,
and then naturally they just become a thing
among their other things.
The possessor becomes the possessed.
Nothing is more rare in any man, says Emerson,
than an act of his own.
But this is just what can be expected
because no one is their own,
no one is themself.

Most people are other people.
They are not living
but only acting roles given to them by others.
Their thoughts are someone else's opinions
and their faces are just masks.
They are faceless.
They have no authentic being at all.
Their lives, a mimicry –
and their passions, a quotation.

Break this vicious circle otherwise you will never _be_.
Break this through meditation –
and it cannot be broken by anything else
because through mind it cannot be broken,
and except for meditation, all else is mind.
Mind is the prison,
meditation, the door.
And the only door.

202.

Love.
Only God is –
that is why it is so difficult to find him.
And God is everywhere –
that is why he seems to be nowhere.
And the seeker is the sought –
that is why all seeking is so futile.

Stop and see.
But the mind is running constantly.
Do not be, and see.
But the mind is trying to be continuously.

Says Auden:
For the garden is the only place there is,
but you will not find it,

until you have looked for it everywhere
and found nowhere that is not a desert.
The miracle is the only thing that happens,
but to you it will not be apparent,
until all events have been studied
and nothing happens that you cannot explain.
And life is the destiny you are bound to refuse
until you have consented to die.

Stop and see.
Do not be, and see.

203.

Love.
Live in the body intimately and deeply.
Feel the body more and let the body feel more.

It is astonishing how many people
are almost completely unaware of themselves physically.
The body is suppressed and denied life too much,
that is why it is just a dead weight and not a living joy.
That is why I insist: go back into the body
and regain the wonderful joy in its movements,
sheer movements.
Make it a meditation and you will be enriched
beyond comprehension.

204.

Love.
John Burroughs remembers:
One day my boy killed what an old hunter told him
was a mock duck.
It looked like a duck,
it acted like a duck,

but when it was placed on the table —
it mocked us!

Remember to make a clearcut distinction
between your self and your mock-selves — the masks,
otherwise in the end they will all mock you!

205.

Love.
Man is strange, very strange,
because he begins by deceiving others
and ends with deceiving himself.

A fakir was walking down the village street
deep in thought
when some urchins began to throw stones at him.
He was taken by surprise,
and besides he was not a big man.

Don't do that, he said, and I will tell you
something of interest to you.

All right, what is it? But no philosophy.

The king is giving a free banquet to all comers —
he simply lied to them.
The children ran off towards the king's palace
as the fakir warmed to his theme —
the delicacies and delights of the entertainment....

He looked up and saw them
disappearing into the distance,
and then suddenly he tucked up his robes ·
and started to sprint after them.
I had better go and see, he panted to himself,
because it *might* be true after all.

206.

Love.
To be religious is to be a yea-sayer:
yes to everything –
yes to life and yes to death,
yes to light and yes to darkness.
Total acceptance is religion.

Says Nicolas De Cusa: Yes God! Yes God!
Yes, yes and always yes.

Say *yes* – and feel it,
and you have entered the temple of the divine.
Say no and you yourself have closed the doors –
or closed yourself to the divine.

No is suicidal, no is poisonous –
know this and be a yea-sayer.
Let your heart say yes with every beat.
Breathe yes in and out
and you will feel the divine all around you
within and without.
He is always present
but he cannot enter through a *no* sign,
He cannot trespass on you.

With a no you are an ego
but with a yes you are just egolessness.
Ego is a Leibnizian monad
without any doors or windows,
and egolessness is *the gate.*
Be a gate –
the divine is waiting to enter you from eternity.

207.

Love.
Begin to live positively – that is,
with positive emotions.
To be negative is to be self-destructive
and ultimately suicidal.

But ordinarily the mind works that way
because it is only an instrument for safety and security;
it detects only death and not life.
So to be completely positive is to transcend mind.

Some fakir was asked to talk to a group
about the negative nature of the mind.
He tacked up on the wall a large sheet of
perfectly white paper.
He made a black spot in the paper with a pencil.
Then he asked each man to say what he saw.
Each man replied: A black spot.
The fakir then said: Yes, there is a little black spot.
But not one of you saw the big expanse of white paper –
and that is the point of my speech.

208.

Love.
The forms of existence are finite – all forms.
Really, to have a form means to be finite.

But existence is infinite
because only the formless can be infinite,
and existence is formlessness,
that is why it can take all forms.

But to take form in any way is to allow death in
because form is a death sentence,

whilst existence itself is eternal life.

Do not be identified with the form:
this identification creates the fear of death
 – in fact, all fear.
Remember the formless
and you will know immortality
because you will be *that – then*.

209.

Love.
One's attitude is everything.

Negative attitudes negate life –
they are good for dying but not good for living.
Life needs positive attitudes;
life feeds on them
because they make you
not only happy but creative also.

Once there lived an old woman,
but the older she became the younger she felt –
because youthfulness has nothing to do with age,
it is an attitude,
and with age and its richness
one can really be younger than the young.
The old woman was so cheerful and creative
that everyone wondered at her.
But you must have some clouds in your life,
said a visitor.
Clouds? she replied. Why, of course:
if there were no clouds
where would the blessed showers come from?

In the presence of trouble –
and there are troubles in life –

the positive mind grows wings
but others buy crutches.

Grow wings, and do not buy crutches.

210.

Love.
There is no security in life
because life cannot exist *except as insecurity* –
that is why the more secure one is
the less alive one becomes.
Death is complete security.
So never be in search of security
because you are searching for death.

To live totally and in ecstasy never demands security.
Accept insecurity blissfully
and when you accept it
then you will know that it has a beauty of its own.

Mulla Nasrudin's tomb
was fronted by an immense wooden door,
barred and padlocked.
Nobody could get into it – at least through the door.
As his last joke
the Mulla decreed that the tomb
should have no walls around it....
What the Mulla did with his tomb
everybody is doing with his life –
and unknowingly!

If you also want to do it –
at least do it knowingly,
because I know that you cannot do it knowingly!
Not only you cannot, but no one can do it,
because no one can knowingly be stupid.

211.

Love.
The universe cares for little but play.
But man in his life does hardly anything but work,
and because of this everything has become upside down.
Hence the agony.

The law, the *tao* of the universe, is play – *leela* –
and the law of human reason is work
because reason cannot think beyond utility.
But existence exists beyond utility.

Meditate on this gap and you will find the bridge –
and the bridge is necessary
because you cannot exist without work,
and to exist only for work is unbearable and unlivable.

The meditative man works
so that he can play more intensely –
the reason for his work is play.
And the unmeditative man plays so that he can work more
efficiently –
the reason for his play is work.

212.

Love.
Life does not need comfort
when it can be offered meaning
nor pleasure when it can be shown purpose,
because in the total intensity of intentional living
is the fruition of the seed of consciousness.
And consciousness without the self is the goal.
Consciousness without the center –
and you have reached.
Consciousness without ego is *nirvana*:

or you may call it God or whatsoever you like.

Know that everyone is seeking this state of being,
but unless the seeker is lost,
this state of being cannot be found –
and the seeker can only be lost
in the fire of total intensity of living.

So live totally.
And live in the moment
and moment to moment,
because there is no other way to live totally,
and no other way to dissolve the center, the self, the ego.

213.

Love.
The secret of meditation is the art of unlearning.
Mind is learning;
meditation is unlearning.
That is – die constantly to your experience.
Don't let it imprison you.
Experience becomes a dead weight
in the living and flowing, riverlike consciousness.

Live in the moment unburdened of the past,
flow in the moment unblocked by the mind,
and you will be in meditation.

Know well that it is innocence that is full
and experience that is empty –
although the surface appearance is quite the contrary.
It is innocence that knows
and experience that knows not –
though innocence never claims
and experience is nothing but claims and claims and claims!
And that is why I say:

innocence is meditation
because it opens the doors of the unknown.

So learn how to unlearn.
So learn how to be beyond the mind.
Do not cling to the known
and the master key will be in your hands.
Be open and vulnerable,
always living and flowing into the unknown,
and you will be in meditation –
you will be meditation.

214.

Love.
Three men made their way to the circle of a Sufi
seeking admission to his teachings.
Almost at once one of them
detached himself from the group,
angered by the erratic behavior of the master.

On the master's instructions
the second was told by a disciple
that the sage was a fraud.
He withdrew soon afterwards.

The third was allowed to talk
but was offered no teaching for so
long that he lost patience and left the circle.

When they had all gone away
the teacher instructed his circle thus:
The first man was an illustration of the principle:
Do not judge fundamental things through seeing.
The second was an illustration of the injunction,
Do not judge things of deep importance
through hearing.

The third was an example of the dictum:
Never judge by speech or the lack of it.

When asked by a disciple
why the applicants could not have been
instructed in this matter
the master retorted: I am here to give real knowledge,
not to teach what people pretend
that they have already learned at their mother's knees.

215.

Love.
Always remember the golden rule: *One step at a time.*

A good natured woman
was often asked for food by tramps.
She finally decided to refuse them;
it was becoming too burdensome.

But shortly after she made her resolution
one young man stopped
and asked her for a little piece of thread.
She noticed that his pants were badly ripped,
that he had a needle,
and she realized he could not get work
with his pants in their present condition,
so she gave him the thread.

The fellow took the thread,
went down the road and sat under a tree
for a few minutes,
then came back to the house.
He told the woman he could not repair the pants
unless he had a piece of cloth for a patch.
She gave him a small piece of material.

About an hour later the young fellow
came again to the house
and said: Madam, these pants are beyond repair.
It would be very good of you
if you could give me a pair of your husband's old pants.
So she gave him a pair of old pants
and smiled at his cleverness.

The young man went behind the barn
and changed into the pants given to him.
Then he returned to the house and told the woman

that the pants were sort of big around the waist,
but if she could give him some food
he was sure they would fit perfectly.

This time the woman burst out laughing
and gave him a big dinner.

And all because he took one step at a time.

216.

Love.
Knowledge is accumulation,
that is why knowledge is always dead,
while learning is moment to moment
because learning is not accumulation but movement.

So do not be dead with knowledge
but move with learning,
only then will you be alive.
Do not be tethered to experience –
experience is slavery.
Always transcend that which has been
so that you are ready to receive the new.
Ecstasy is always with the new,
with the fresh, with the young,
with the discontinuous –
and to be always in the discontinuous
is to be in the divine.

217.

Love.
If one is aware of the present moment
then one also becomes aware of the fact that
there is no *me* inside.

The me is my past,
the me is the dead past.
The me is not my life because it is not living.
The ego can exist only in the past
or in the future –
which is nothing but a projection of the past.
That is why awareness, moment to moment awareness,
leads to egolessness –
because *the ego cannot exist in the present*
and because awareness cannot exist except in the present.
So they cannot exist simultaneously.

Ego is unawareness
and awareness is egolessness.

218.

Love.
I live without planning,
and I also feel that this is the only way to be alive at all.
In fact I live a wild life,
absolutely unplanned,
not knowing anything about the future –
not even about the next moment.
Today is enough for me –
really more than enough!
The moment that is present is the only living moment –
the past is dead in the sense that it is no more
and the future is also dead
in the sense that it is not yet born.
And so to be concerned with the past is to be dead
and to be concerned with the future is also to be dead.
The only way to be alive is to be here and now –
in the moment and totally in it.
Living moment to moment
I have found that ecstasy and bliss
which is not of this world at all.

The single moment lived totally transcends time itself.
It becomes the gap between two moments of time,
and if one can be in this gap
then one is beyond death
because time is death
and timelessness is life.
Life is not something fixed and finished,
life is living what is,
a process, just riverlike,
flowing always into the unknown,
from the shores of the known to the shores
of the unknown.

219.

Love.
Anger, violence, greed or envy
cannot be overcome by the cultivation of their opposites,
because anger itself will cultivate its opposite
and violence will be present in its cultivated non-violence.
So always be aware of the hypnotic spell of the opposite:
it never solves any problem
because it is beating around the bush.

Do not fall into the trap of the opposite
but understand anger, violence or greed
or anything else
directly.
To seek the opposite is a way of escape.
To seek the opposite is cowardice.

Live with your mind as it is.
Do not try to change it.
Be brave and face it and understand it.

When the light of awareness falls on anger or
greed or envy

there is change.
Awareness acts as a catalytic agent –
and then anger does not change into its opposite,
it is not that violence becomes non-violence,
but there is *no-anger*,
there is *no-violence*.
And when there is no-violence there is *no-mind*,
and an altogether different dimension opens its door:
the dimension of the spontaneous,
the dimension of the divine.

220.

Love.
Moment to moment life passes into death,
because it is death.
Covered, it appears as life,
uncovered it is death.
Always remember this fact.
This is silent meditation.

And when this remembering even penetrates
your dreams
you will have a new door opened unto you.
In fact through it you will be altogether new,
and ultimately reborn.
Remembering death gives a new dimension
to consciousness
because to remember death is not natural.
On the contrary nature has arranged
that one should not be aware of it
because the moment one transcends death
one transcends nature also.
And one cannot transcend death
unless one is totally aware of the fact.
So be totally aware of death.
And it is happening each moment within and without.

It is present everywhere.
And because it is so obvious one becomes absent to it.
Remember – and deepen the consciousness,
because as the awareness of death goes deeper
one becomes capable of feeling that which is deathless.

Really, death is the door –
the opening to the deathless.
But be conscious of it.
Be conscious and transcend.
Be conscious and know that which is before birth and after
death.
And – you are that.

221.

Love.
Be a stranger to yourself.
See life as a river flowing through time.
Stand on the bank, neither curious nor concerned.
Glance or gaze at the driftwood of your past
floating in your memory –
just like the incidents one reads about in the paper.
Detached and indifferent
remember that nothing matters.
Only exist –
and the explosion.

222.

Love.
Always be positive, in each and every situation –
that helps meditative awareness very much.
Negative attitudes negate the whole effort.

Diogenes was looking for an honest man in New Delhi.

Any luck? asked a wayfarer.
Oh, pretty fair, sir, replied Diogenes.
I still have my lantern.

223.

Love.
Philosophy cannot cure you of questions –
on the contrary, it can give you more.
I heard this at a chemist's shop:

Did the patent medicine you purchased cure your aunt?

Good heavens, no.
On reading the wrapper around the bottle
she got two more diseases.

224.

Love.
Mulla Nasrudin was carrying home some liver
which he had just bought.
In the other hand he held a recipe for liver pie
which a friend had given him.
Suddenly a buzzard swooped down
and carried off the liver.
You fool! shouted Nasrudin.
Having the meat is all very well,
but what will you do without the recipe?

225.

Love.
Man can only know what God is not.
To know what God is, is impossible

because that's where the realm of *being begins.*
You cannot know God but you can *be,*
and in that dimension is the only knowing.
But *that* knowing
is altogether different from all our other knowing
because in that knowing there is no knower
and no known,
but only *knowing.*

That is why in that dimension knowing and being
are the same.

There is even no knowledge.
because knowledge is dead and therefore a thing.
Moreover, knowledge is always of the past,
and God is never in the past
or in the future.
God is *now,* always now;
and *here,* and always here.

Close your eyes and *see.*
Then open your eyes and see.
Then neither close your eyes nor open your eyes and see.

226.

Love.
There was once a man
who was obsessed with the idea
that there was a secret knower in those
who achieved success.

To discover this secret
he devoted years to study and research:
ancient masonry, philosophy, astrology, psychology,
salesmanship, religious beliefs,
the various cults that have had their rise and fall.

All these he studied long and diligently,
but no conclusion was visible.
He struggled and struggled
but still there was no conclusion.
And then instead of success in his search
for the secret of success
came death – and as death approached him
he realized the goal of his whole life's efforts,
and finally he gave his conclusion to those
who were near him.
It came in two short words: *I will.*

227.

Love.
Do not believe in thinking
because that is the greatest of all superstitions –
but well hidden
because it pretends to be anti-superstitious!

Thinking is nothing but dust in a blind mind
because you cannot think that which is not known –
and you need not think that which is already known.

The encounter is always with the _unknown_.
The unknown is everywhere,
within and without,
and thinking is always in the known and of the known.
You can never be in contact with the unknown
through the known
so throw the known and be in contact with the unknown.

And this is what I call meditation.

228.

Love.
Man goes on dreaming and desiring
but basically remains where he is,
and in the end
nothing but the ashes of his dreams and desires
are in his hands –
and of course there are tears in his eyes.

Panchatantra has a beautiful story:
In a certain town lived a Brahmin named Seedy
who got some barley meal by begging,
ate a portion,
and filled a jar with the remainder.

This jar he hung on a peg one night,
placed his cot beneath it
and fixing his gaze on the jar
fell into a hypnotic reverie.
Well, here is a jar of barley meal, he thought.
Now if a famine comes
I will get a hundred rupees for it.
With that sum I will get two she-goats:
every six months they will bear two more she-goats.
After goats, cows.
When the cows calve I will sell the calves.
After cows, buffalos.
After buffalos, mares.
From the mares I shall get plenty of horses.
The sale of these will mean plenty of gold.
The gold will buy a great house with an inner court.
Then someone will come to my house
and offer his lovely daughter with a dowry
She will bear a son whom I shall call Moonlord.
When he is old enough to ride on my knee
I will take a book,
sit on the stable roof and think.
Just then Moonlord will see me,
will jump from his mother's lap
in his eagerness to ride on my knee
and will go too near the horses.
Then I shall get angry and tell my wife to take the boy
but she will be too busy with her chores
and will not pay attention to what I say.
Then I will get up and kick her!

Being sunk in his hypnotic dream
he let fly such a kick that he smashed the jar
and the barley meal it contained made him white all over.

229.

Love.
Go on discarding: not this, not this *(neti, neti),*
and ultimately when nothing remains to be discarded –
then the explosion happens.
Do not cling to anything, to any thought.

Go on and on until the *nothingness.*

I have heard about a little boy, Toyo,
and his meditations.
He was only twelve years old
but he wanted to be given something to ponder on,
to meditate on,
so one evening he went to Mokurai, the Zen master,
struck the gong softly to announce his presence,
and sat before the master in respectful silence.
Finally the master said:
Toyo, show me the sound of two hands.
Toyo clapped his hands.
Good, said the master.
Now show me the sound of one hand clapping.
Toyo was silent.
Finally he bowed and left to meditate on the problem.

The next night he returned and struck the gong
with one palm.
That is not right, said the master.
The next night Toyo returned and played geisha music with one
hand.
That is not right, said the master.
Again and again Toyo returned with some answer
but the master said again and again, That is not right.

For nights Toyo tried new sounds
but each and every answer was rejected.
The question itself was absurd

so no answer could be right.
When Toyo came on the eleventh night,
before he said anything the master said:
That is still not right!
 – then he stopped coming to the master.

For a year he thought of every possible sound
and discarded them all,
and when there was nothing left to be discarded any more
he exploded into enlightenment.

When he was no more, he returned to the master
and without striking the gong he sat down and bowed.
He was not saying anything
and there was silence.
Then the master said:
So you have heard the sound without sound!

230.

Love.
Thought is divisive,
it divides ad *infinitum*,
so thought can never come to the total, to the *whole*.
And the *whole* is while the parts are not –
or they are only for the mind –
and if there is no mind then there are no parts.

With the mind and because of the mind
the *one* becomes many – or appears so;
and with the mind and through the mind,
to conceive the *one is* impossible.

Of course it can think about the *one*,
but that one is nothing but a putting together of
all the parts,
and that one is quite different from the *one* which is.

The one which is conceptualized by the mind
is just a mathematical construct:
it is not a living whole,
it is not organic,
and unless one experiences the cosmos as
an organic whole
one has not known anything at all.

This is not possible with thought,
but this is possible with _no-thought_.

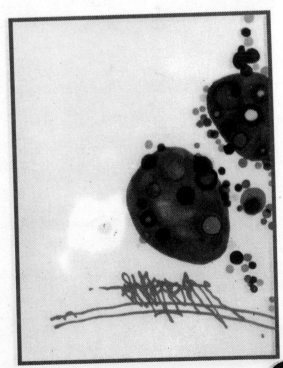

231.

Love.
Emptiness is all —
and to get hold of emptiness is to attain all and be all.
But it is very arduous to get hold of emptiness —
because it is emptiness! And it hurts much —
though it is emptiness, it still hurts much!
Because to make way for it *the ego has to die.*
But I am happy that you are dying
because this is the only way to be beyond death —
I say: the only way.
Remember this always.

Sekkyo once said to one of his monks:
Can you get hold of emptiness?

I will try, said the monk;
and he cupped his hands in the air.

That is absurd, said Sekkyo.
You have not got anything in there.

Well, master, said the monk,
please show me the right way.

Thereupon Sekkyo seized the monk's nose
and gave it a great yank.

Ouch! yelled the monk. You hurt me!

I cannot help it,
because that is the only way to get hold of emptiness!
said Sekkyo.

232.

Love.
Man asks questions and then answers them himself.
Nothing is answered in this way.
But man is capable of deceiving himself –
and the whole of philosophy
is nothing but such a deception.
Man asks: What is mind?
And then answers himself: Not matter?
And then asks: What is matter?
And then answers: Not mind?
And this stupid game goes on.

I have heard about a distinguished philosopher
who always began his speeches with: Why are we here?
He had occasion to address the inmates
of a mental hospital
and ended with: Ladies and Gentlemen, why are we here?
One of the inmates called out:
We are all here because we are not all there!

233.

Love.
The mind always thinks in terms of the self.
It is egocentric.

During the French revolution
a man from Paris stopped at a village
and was asked by a friend what was happening.
They are cutting off heads by the thousands,
said the visitor.
How terrible! cried the villager.
That could ruin my hat business!

But this is the way of the mind,

and because of this it is never in tune with the cosmos,
so how can it know *life?*
It cannot know it because it cannot be one with it.
Really with the mind there is no knowing
but only superficial acquaintance.
Intimate and deep knowing comes only with no-mind –
and meditation is the dissolving of mind into no-mind.

234.

Love.
A monk asked Hyakujo Yekai:
What is the most miraculous event in the world?
Hyakujo said: I sit here *all by myself!*

235.

Love.
Freedom *from* becoming means freedom *for* being.
Becoming is desiring,
being is *that which* is.
Becoming is longing for the future,
being is to be in the present.
Becoming is mental,
being is existential.
That is why becoming must cease for the being
to reveal itself.

Becoming is just like the smoke around the flame,
or just like the outer covering around the seed,
so please let the smoke go
for the flame to explode in its complete glory
and splendor,
and let the seed die to its outer shell
so that it may be what it is in its innermost depth.

236.

Love.
No more principles are needed.
The world is already much too burdened with principles
and people who are men of principle.

I have heard that once a priest was consoling a widow.
He said with much feeling that her dead husband
was a man of principle.
That he was, sighed the widow.
Every Saturday night for these past twenty years
the poor man would come home
and faithfully hand me his pay envelope –
he never missed doing that.
Of course the envelope was always empty,
but mind you,
he was loyal to the principle of the thing.

237.

Love.
Religion is – living without conflict,
that is, without ideas
and without ideals,
because whenever one lives with ideals
there is conflict,
there is conflict between
that which is and that which should be,
and then life is misery.

See this and go beyond.
In fact the very seeing of the fact is going beyond.
And please do not ask the seemingly inevitable, "*How?*"
Because there is no *how* to it.
Either you see it or you do not see it –
and moreover the how again creates conflict.

238.

Love.
Bhakti needs only time to absorb the shock she
has come across
in her deep meditations;
remember – only time and nothing else.

The shock is nothing new.
It happens whenever the deeper layers of the unconscious are
encountered.
Before any mutation this is absolutely necessary.
Be grateful to the divine because this is a good omen.
Bhakti needed it badly,
and when she is out of it she will be a totally new person.
Soon she will be twice-born.

At present she is passing through a great spiritual crisis,
so you be with her – *but just as if you are not.*
Be present, but with absolute absence.
This is the only way you can be helpful to her.

Let her be alone as much as possible. Do not talk with her
except where it is needed absolutely,
and then too be telegraphic.
But if she herself wants to talk
let her talk as much as she likes,
and you yourself just be a passive listener.

Let her do whatsoever she wants to do or not do
and soon everything will be okay.
Do not worry at all.
I will always be there beside you –
and if you can see, you will be able to see me also.

Of course Bhakti will feel my presence
and become aware of me so many times in these days.
Convey my blessings to her.

239.

Love.
One day a man came to the Sufi teacher, Bahaudin.
He asked for help in his problems
and guidance on the path.
Bahaudin told him to abandon spiritual studies
and to leave his court at once.

A kind-hearted visitor began to remonstrate
with Bahaudin.
You shall have a demonstration, said the master.
At that moment a bird flew into the room
darting hither and thither,
not knowing where to go in order to escape.
The master waited until the bird settled
near the only open window
of the chamber and then suddenly clapped his hands.
Alarmed, the bird flew straight
through the opening of the window
to freedom.
To him that sound must have been something of a shock,
even an affront, do you not agree? said Bahaudin.

240.

Love.
Fu Ta Shih says:
Each night one embraces a Buddha while sleeping,
each morning one gets up again with him.
Rising or sitting –
both watch and follow one another
Speaking or not speaking –
they are in the same place.
They never part even for a moment
but are like the body and its shadow.
If you wish to know the Buddha's whereabouts,

in the sound of your own voice
there he is.

Do you understand this?
If not now – when will you understand?

And this is not being asked for the first time,
but many many times in many many lives
the same question has been raised –
and you have not yet answered!

Now, is it not time enough?

241.

Love.
Mind is localization of consciousness,
and it can be localized in any part of the body.
Ordinarily we have localized it in the head,
but other cultures and other civilizations in the past
have tried other parts of the body also,
and on other planets
there are beings with other parts of their bodies
working as their minds.
But whatsoever the part chosen
localization of consciousness means its freezing,
and whenever it ceases to flow freely as is needed
it is no longer consciousness in its suchness.
Meditation means: consciousness *in its suchness*.
So let consciousness fill the whole body,
let it flow throughout the totality of your being
and you will have a feeling of aliveness
which is never known and felt
by localized consciousness.
Whenever there is localization of consciousness
the part in which the localization happens
becomes tense and diseased

and the remainder of the body becomes a dead weight.
But with meditative consciousness
or flowing consciousness
everything changes completely:
the whole body becomes alive, sensitive and aware
and consequently weightless.
Then there is no center at which
tensions can exist and accumulate:
they cannot exist without frozen blocks of consciousness.
The flowing, moving consciousness
washes them out constantly with every movement.
And when the whole body is alive
only then do you begin to feel
the cosmic consciousness all around you.
How can a frozen consciousness,
and that too surrounded by a dead body,
feel the cosmic?

242.

Love.
Now man knows more about man than ever
and yet no problem is solved.
It seems that something is basically wrong
with our so-called knowledge itself.

This whole knowledge is derived from analysis,
and analysis is incapable of penetrating
the depths of consciousness.

The analytical method is all right for matter
or for things
because there is no _inside to them,_
but consciousness is _insideness,_
and to use the analytical method with consciousness
is to treat it as an object,
while it is not an object at all.

And it cannot be made an object;
its very nature is subjectivity,
its being is subjectivity,
so it must not be approached from outside
because then whatsoever is known about it is not about it.
Consciousness must be approached from inside –
and then the method is meditation and not analysis.

Meditation is synthetic:
it is concerned with the whole and not with the parts,
it is subjective and not objective,
it is irrational or super-rational and not rational,
it is religious or mystic and not scientific.

Authentic knowledge of consciousness
comes only through meditation and all else is
just superficial acquaintance
and basically erroneous
because the very source of it is fallacious and poisonous.

243.

Love.
Life is a dream so enjoy it;
but do not ask for more because
then you only disturb the dream
and get nothing except a disturbed night.
Be a witness to the dreaming mind
and then there is transcendence:
then you go beyond dreaming and beyond mind itself.

And know well that there is an awakening
below the dreaming mind
which is nothing but just a disturbed dream.
One can get to this below-dreaming state of awakening
through asking for more, desiring more –
as ordinarily we all do.

In a dream Mulla Nasrudin saw himself
being counted out coins
and when there were nine silver pieces in his hand
the invisible donor stopped giving them.
Nasrudin shouted: *I must have ten!* so loudly
that he woke himself up.
Finding that all the money had disappeared
he closed his eyes again and murmured,
All right, then, give them back –
I will take the nine.

There is also an awakening above the dreaming mind –
the real awakening
in comparison to which man ordinarily is asleep.
One can reach this awakening
through *witnessing* the dreaming mind –
and unless one reaches it one is not really alive.

244.

Love.
The divine is that from which one cannot depart,
and that from which one can depart is not the divine.

So find that from which you have never departed
and cannot ever depart from –
and then laugh at the absurdity of the human mind
and its efforts!

Buddha is still laughing because of that.
Listen!

245.

Love.
Why does man suffer?
Man suffers because of his craving,
craving to possess that which cannot be possessed,
and craving to keep things forever with himself
which are essentially impermanent.
And chief among these things is his own ego,
his own *persona*.
But all things are impermanent.
Except for change itself
everything changes.
Really nothing is
because everything is only a process,
so as soon as one tries to possess anything it slips away.
The possessor himself is slipping away constantly!
Then there is frustration
and then there is suffering.
Know this well,
realize this well and there will be no suffering
because then you have unearthed the root.

246.

Love.
The self can never be free –
because the self itself is the bondage.
This is the meaning of the penetrating saying of Jesus:
He that saveth his life shall lose it
and he that loseth his life shall know life abundant.
Or that of Lao Tzu in *Tao-te-Ching*:
He who humbles himself shall be saved,
he who bends shall be made straight,
and he who empties himself shall be filled.
One is not to make the self free;
rather on the contrary, *one has to be free from the self*.

The self is nothing but the husk of the seed.
Do not cling to it.
Sings Wu Ming Fu:
The seed that has to grow must lose itself as a seed,
and they that creep may be transformed
through the chrysalis to wings.
Wilt thou then, O mortal, cling to husks
which wrongly seem to you to be the self?

247.

Love.
The gates of the temple are wide open
and it is only after thousands of years
that such opportunity comes to this earth.
Know well that they will not remain open forever.
The opportunity can be lost very easily,
and you are still wavering,
and you are still hesitating –
to enter or not to enter,
to be or not to be.

I know that the challenge is great, but I know also
that your being is completely ready to take the jump.
Hence my insistent call for you to come and enter.

And this is not for the first time that I have called you,
nor the first life;
I know you, Bhakti, through so many births!
And soon you will also remember many things.
But not before the jump.

Only your superficial *persona* is resisting, not you –
and it is expected to resist always
because the moment one takes the plunge
into the unknown
it has to die naturally.

So please do not identify yourself with it;
be a witness to it, and you will be in the jump.
It is time now to die to the old ego
and be reborn to the supreme self!

248.

Love.
Logic is not all;
nor is consistency;
because even madness has its own methods,
rationalizations and inner consistencies.

A madman was throwing handfuls
of crumbs around his house.
What are you doing? someone asked him.
Keeping the elephants away, he answered.
But there are no elephants in these parts,
said the enquirer.
That's right – my method is effective, isn't it?
declared the madman.

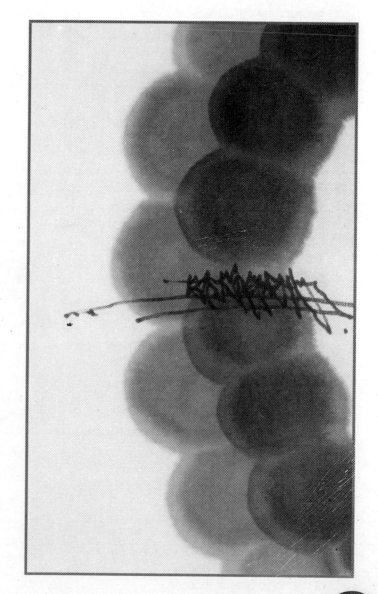

249.

Love.
Total acceptance of existence is impossible for the mind
because the mind exists as denial.

It exists with the *no*,
and with a total *yes* it dies.
So it continues to find reasons to say no
even if there are no reasons.

Walking with a disciple one day
Mulla Nasrudin saw for the first time in his life
a beautiful lakeland scene.
What a delight! he exclaimed. But if only, if only....
If only what, master? asked the disciple.
If only they had not put water in it! said the Mulla.

250.

Love.
Meditation is like the sea:
receiving the dirty river and yet remaining pure.
You need not be purified before it,
but you will come out of it purified.

Meditation is unconditional,
purity is not a prerequisite but a consequence.

251.

Love.
Be as if dead,
and then dualisms will not contaminate you
and you will reach the state
of the non-arising of thought.

The brightness of self-nature will appear in full –
and when this happens you are no more.

This disappearance is the appearance of the divine,
so please – *disappear!*

252.

Love.
Existence exists in order to exist –
and likewise life.
There is no meaning to it beyond itself
so never posit any meaning,
otherwise you will feel its meaninglessness.
It is not meaningless and it cannot be so
because there is no meaning in it all!

The very search for meaning is mean and ugly
because it comes from the utilitarian mind of man.

Existence simply is and likewise life:
there is no purpose in it and there is no end to it.
Feel it here and now!
Please do not practice it
because that is the way of the utilitarian mind.
Be playful and only then will you know the playfulness
of the universe.

And to know that is to be religious.

253.

Love.
Do not continue moving in the old rut –
and the way out is just by your hand.
The mind is the past, the dead past;

one has to break it somewhere and jump out of it
The mind is the prison, the slavery.
Be free of it.
And the moment is ripe.

Of course I know that you are still not clearly aware of it
but you are not unaware either.
Gather courage and jump into the unknown.
Just one step is enough
because the next follows it automatically.

But do not go on thinking and thinking and thinking.
Thinking promises to lead you somewhere
but the promise remains always a promise,
because thinking is just impotent
as far as life is concerned.
So please, be existential.
Do not hesitate.
And you have nothing to lose – because you
have nothing!
Realize this and be *nothing – no-one.*

254.

Love.
Life is movement,
process,
fluidity;
but ideas become fixed,
so they become also anti-life.
They become dead blocks.
Do not remain with them.
Move.
And do not fear inconsistency
because life is not a syllogism,
life is not a theory
but a mystery.

Someone asked Mulla Nasrudin:
How old are you, Mulla?
Forty.
But you said the same last time I asked you, five years ago!
Yes, I am always consistent and always stand by
what I have said.

255.

Love.
Mind means consciousness somewhere –
centered,
focused and tense.

Meditation means consciousness nowhere,
and when it is nowhere it is everywhere –
decentralized.
Unfocused and non-tense.
Mind is agony by its very nature,
meditation – ecstasy.

Do not treat consciousness like a cat tied to a string.
This very treatment –
or mistreatment –
creates the mind.
The consciousness must be left to itself, utterly free
to move and be
according to its nature.
Do not localize it.
Do not be partial.
This is the essence of my discipline of no-discipline.

Preserve the absolute fluidity of your consciousness
and then you will not be,
and when you are not and only consciousness is
then for the first time the doors of the divine
are open to you.

256.

Love.
Yes, man learns by experience!

Two old drunkards
were in the habit of coming together twice a week
to the wine-seller to get drunk.

After years of this one of them died.
His old friend came in on the Saturday
and they told him his pal had died –
that the whisky had been taken into blood circulation
and so saturated his blood and his breath
that one night before going to bed
the old man went to blow out the candle
and his breath caught fire and he was burned to death.
The other man promptly called for a Bible
and took an oath that from that time forward
he would never blow out another candle in his life!

Yes, man learns by experience!

257.

Love.
Do not imitate anyone,
do not follow anyone,
otherwise you will be just a pseudo existence –
and that is worse than suicide.
Be yourself –
and only then
can you be responsible
and authentic and real.
But ordinarily everyone is just secondhand and borrowed,
and that makes everything ugly.

Mulla Nasrudin went to a mosque and sat down.
His shirt was rather short
and the man behind him pulled it lower,
thinking it looked unseemly.
Nasrudin immediately pulled the shirt of the man
in front of him.
What are you doing? asked the man in front.
Don't ask me, ask the man behind – he started it, said Nasrudin.

258.

Love.
The real religious experience
cannot be organized, taught or transmitted.
To systematize it is to kill it.
It is so living and moving and dynamic
that to impose a pattern on it is impossible;
and the experience is always so unique and individual
that it cannot be put into any category –
although it happens when the individual is not.
It cannot be followed,
for everyone has to find it for himself,
and that is the beauty of it,
and also its freedom and virginity.
It is not new in the sense of any opposition to the old,
it is new in the sense of timelessness –
that is, eternally fresh and innocent –
as every flower is new
and every sunrise is new
and every love is new.
It is not borrowed from the past,
it is not based on any tradition,
it is not derived from without,
it happens within,
without any causality.
It happens unconditionally.
It is not continuous with the mind,

it is a discontinuous explosion.
There are clouds in the sky
and the sky cannot be seen,
but there is no causal chain.
The clouds have gone
and the sky is clear
but there is no cause-and-effect relationship.
The sky has not even known the clouds!
It has not been affected by them in any way whatsoever.

259.

Love.
Life becomes more authentic
in the direct encountering of death.
But we always try to escape the fact of death,
and so life becomes pseudo and phony.
Even death, when authentic, has a beauty of its own
while pseudo-life is just ugly.

Meditate on death
because there is no way to know life
unless you stand face to face with death.
And it is everywhere;
wherever life is death is also.
They are really two aspects of one and the same phenomenon,
and when one comes to know this, one transcends both.

Only in that transcendence
is the total flowering of consciousness and the ecstasy of being.

260.

Love.
Man adds everything to his ego —
while everything goes on without him.

He is nothing,
but he thinks himself everything.

Mulla Nasrudin was walking past a well
when he had the impulse to look into it.
It was night, and as he peered
into the deep water
he saw the moon's reflection there.
I must save the moon! the Mulla thought,
otherwise she will never wane
and the fasting month of Ramajan
will never come to an end.
He found a rope, threw it in and called down:
Hold tight! Keep bright, help is at hand!
The rope caught in a rock inside the well
and Nasrudin heaved as hard as he could.
Straining back he suddenly felt the rope give way
as it became loose and he was thrown on his back.
As he lay there panting
he saw the moon riding in the sky above.
Glad to be of service, said Nasrudin.
Just as well I came along, wasn't it?

261.

Love.
Are you really aware of what anger is?
Are you really aware of it when it is present?
I ask these questions
because man is *never present in the present.*
Man lives in the past
and only becomes aware of anything
when it has become a part of his memory.

One becomes aware of anger and sadness
only when they are all over,
and then awareness is just pseudo-awareness;

it is not awareness but remembering,
and remembering leads nowhere
because it is running in a circle.
Then one can fight with anger
but can never understand it,
and fighting with anger is anger –
of course more subtle
and therefore more strong and more poisonous.

So do not think about anger or sadness or happiness
and do not understand remembrance to be awareness
but be aware *when anger* is present.
Be totally conscious of it,
live it consciously and do not escape from it
and then you will know what it is.
To understand it is to transcend it.
Then you will find a silence descending on you
which passes all understanding.

262.

Love.
Never to have seen the truth
is better than to have seen it
and not to have acted on it.

263.

Love.
One should never be afraid of rising thoughts or desires
but only of the delay in being aware of them.

264.

Love.
The purest ore is produced from the hottest furnace;
and the brook would lose its song
if we removed the rocks.

265.

Love.
Be empty and you will know.
Be empty and you will be the mirror.
Only total nothingness is capable of knowing all!

I have heard that the nun Chiyono studied for years
and meditated for years on the ultimate questions
of existence
but was unable to find the light.
The thinking was filling her so much
that she could not be a passage for the divine.
She was so filled with herself
that she could not be a host to the divine guest,
and the more she longed for enlightenment
the further off it was.
But one moonlit night she was carrying an old pail
filled with water
  – and the thing happened!
She was watching the full moon reflected
in her pail of water
when the bamboo strip that held the pail staves broke.
The pail fell all apart,
the water ran out,
the moon's reflection disappeared –
and with it Chiyono herself disappeared.
She was not – but the enlightenment was there!

She wrote this verse:

This way and that way
I tried to keep the pail together,
hoping the weak bamboo would never break.
But suddenly the bottom fell out:
no more water
no more moon in the water –
and emptiness in my hand!

266.

Love.
One day Lin-chi was asked:
What is the essence of meditation?
Lin-chi came right down from his seat
and taking hold of the questioner
by the front of his robe,
slapped his face, then let him go.
The questioner, of course, stood there stupefied.

Then Lin-chi laughed and said to him:
Why don't you bow?
This woke him from his reverie,
and when he was about to make a bow to the master
he had his first taste of meditation!

Please read this again and again and again,
and if you do not have the same taste
then slap your face yourself
then laugh and bow down to yourself –
and then you will certainly have the same taste.

267.

Love.
The sun is rising high in the sky.
Its light enters the house through an opening.

The dust is seen moving in the ray of light
but the empty space of the room is unmoving.

Now close your eyes and be silent.
Then ask yourself: Who am I –
the moving dust or the unmoving space of the room?

Do not answer intellectually,
because intellectual answers are not answers,
but *wait and realize*.

Hsu Yun says: The mind is nothing but foreign dust.

Who are you – the mind? – the foreign dust? or – ?

268.

Love.
The mind exists to raise questions,
but only questions.
It never answers,
and it can never answer.
That is beyond it,
it is not meant for that,
that is not its function.
But it *tries* to answer,
and the result is the mess called philosophy!

Meditation never questions,
but it answers.
It is the answer,
because it is life,
because it is existence.

Question – and there is no answer.
Do not question – and you are the answer.

Why is it so?
It is so because
the questioning consciousness, *mind*, is disturbed,
and the non-questioning consciousness, *no-mind*,
is silent, quiet and at rest in its suchness.

Philosophy comes out of questioning,
religion, out of the non-questioning consciousness.
Logic is the method of philosophy
and meditation the method of religion.

269.

Love.
If the present is just continuous with the past

then it is not present at all.
To be present,
the present must be discontinuous with the past,
only then is it young, fresh and new –
and then it is not a part of time
but is eternity itself.

The *now* is eternal
but we live in the past or in the future –
which is nothing but a faint echo of the past itself.
Our whole activity springs from the past
or the future –
which is the same thing.
Then the present is false and dead:
and if the present is false then we cannot be real,
and if the present is dead then we cannot be alive.
That is why I insist on living in the present
and dying each moment to the past.

Live atomically – moment to moment –
and then your life will have a totally different quality:
the quality of the divine.

270.

Love.
To me meditation means –
be playful and transcend all seriousness.
See: life is not serious.
Look around: existence is not serious.
Only disease is serious, and of course death,
and the exploiters of death – the priests!
Life is playful and festive and therefore purposeless.
It is not going anywhere, because there is nowhere to go.
It is always *here* and *here.*
It is always *now* and *now.*
It is just abundant energy overflowing from here to here

and from now to now,
and once you know it and be it
you are in that ecstasy which is the purpose
of purposelessness!
Don't be a *mind* and you will know it and be it.
Meditation is no-mindedness.
Mind is thinking, and thinking is going astray
from the *being*.
Mind is forgetfulness of "that which is".
Meditation is *coming back home.*
So, come back home.
And I create situations so that
you may remember the forgotten,
and I will go on creating situations
until you have returned.

271.

Love.
There are things which cannot be proved,
and there is no evidence for them
because they are self-evident.
To try to prove them is ridiculous,
and the effort shows that one
is not acquainted with them.
Such are all the proofs of God.

Sitting one day in the teahouse
Mulla Nasrudin heard the rhetoric of
a traveling scholar –
he was arguing to prove the existence of God.
Questioned by one of the company on some point
the scholar drew a book from his pocket
and slammed it on the table:
This is my evidence. *And* I wrote it myself!
A man who could not only read but write was a rarity,
and a man who had written a book...!

The villagers treated the pundit with profound respect –
and of course Mulla Nasrudin was impressed.

Some days later Mulla appeared at the teahouse
and asked whether anyone wanted to buy a house.
Tell us something about it,
Mulla, the people asked him,
for we did not even know that
you had a house of your own.
Actions speak louder than words! shouted Mulla,
and from his pocket he took a brick
and hurled it on the table in front of them.
This is my evidence!
Examine the quality –
and I built the house myself!

272.

Love.
When you are with me be completely at ease and relaxed;
that is, be totally yourself.
If you feel like crying, then cry;
if you feel like weeping, then weep –
but just be continually aware.

Do not think about what you are doing,
just be the doing.
And when your senses are shaken
like leaves in the wind,
enter this shaking,
because only in such situations is the being revealed.

If a feeling against someone or for someone arises
do not project it on the person in question
but remain centered in yourself,
and you will know a transcendence
which is not of this world at all.

273.

Love.
The past is not
nor is the future,
but the mind exists between these two non-existences,
and therefore – the misery.

To live in the mind is to live in misery,
in agony and in hell.
The mind is the hell.
Be aware *suddenly* of this
and then there is a new opening:
the opening of the present,
the opening of that-which-is.
The present is the only existence
or, it is the existence.
Be in it and you are liberated.
Live in it and there is bliss.

274.

Love.
No ideology can help to create a new world
or a new mind
or a new human being,
because ideological orientation itself
is the root cause of all the conflicts and all the miseries.
Thought creates boundaries,
thought creates divisions
and thought creates prejudices.
Thought itself cannot bridge them;
that is why all ideologies fail.
Now man must learn to live without ideologies:
religious, political or otherwise.
When the mind is not tethered to any ideology
it is free to move to new understandings.

And in that freedom flowers all that is good
and all that is beautiful.

275.

Love.
A disciple of Rinzai met a party
of three men on a bridge.
One of the three asked him:
How deep is the river of meditation?
Find out for yourself, he said,
and offered to throw the questioner from the bridge.
But unfortunately the man ran away from him in time
and escaped.

If you meet such a man, who can throw you in the river,
be fortunate enough to be thrown!

And you have met such a man!
Now be *thrown*.

276.

Love.
You possess only that which will not be lost in death.
All else is illusion –
even the possessor,
because that too will not be able to stand the final shipwreck.

Then find out what is left.
Turn in and meditate.
Discard all that is vulnerable to death.
Say: Not this, not that,
and go deep to the point
where nothing more remains to be discarded
 – and *the illumination*.

277.

Love.
Nothing great is ever accomplished without going mad,
that is, without breaking through
the ordinary level of consciousness
and letting loose the hidden powers lying further below,
and also penetrating to the realm that is further above.

And it may not be true for any other great thing,
but it is absolutely true as far as meditation is concerned.
Meditation means *madness* –
of course, with a method!

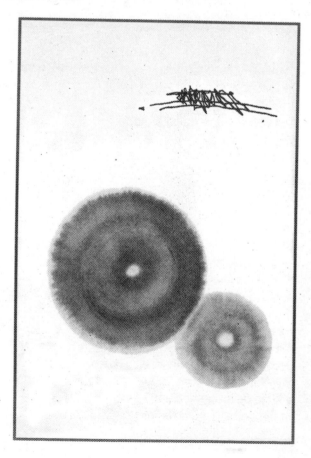

278.

Love.
Detach yourself from all fixed ideas:
they are the killers of all aliveness and innocence –
which are musts for illumination.
Beware of the trap of preconceptions;
they make a stagnant pool of your consciousness,
and to meet the ocean you need a dynamic one.
Be alive and fluid and flowing –
then the goal is not far off.

279.

Love.
Meditation is the disciplined opening of the self to God.
Because of fear we are closed, and only love
can become a door.
So love more –
or rather be loving, then there is less fear and less tension,
and you are more open.
This helps meditation as nothing else.
Meditation plus love is the path.

280.

Love.
Truth is never secondhand,
it cannot be transferred.
One has to know it and be it oneself.
That is why all tradition falsifies it,
and all scriptures, and all words,
and in the end it is nothing
but the soup of Mulla Nasrudin....

But first I must tell you the story.

A relative from the country
came to see Nasrudin and brought a duck.
Nasrudin was grateful,
had the bird cooked, and shared it with the guest.
Presently another visitor arrived.
I am a friend, he said, of the man who gave you the duck.
Nasrudin fed him as well.
This happened several times.
Nasrudin's house had become like a restaurant
for out-of-town visitors.
Everyone was a friend of the friend
of the original donor of the duck.
Finally Nasrudin was exasperated.
One day there was a knock at the door and
a stranger appeared.
I am the friend of the friend of the friend of the man
who brought you the duck from the country, he said.
Come in, said Nasrudin.
They seated themselves at the table
and Nasrudin asked his wife to bring the soup.
When the guest tasted it
it seemed to be nothing more than warm water.
What sort of soup is this? he asked the Mulla.
That, said Nasrudin,
is the soup of the soup of the soup of the soup
of the duck.

281.

Love.
Man is not a rational animal,
but only a rationalizing one;
and that is more dangerous than just being irrational.

Give me a shot of bourbon and a shot of water –
said the obviously heavy drinker to the bartender.
When the order was placed before him on the bar

the lush pulled a worm from his pocket
and dropped it into the glass of water.
After watching it swim around for a few seconds
the man drew the worm from the water
and dropped it into the whisky.
It wriggled briefly, then curled up and died.
You see that? said the lush to the bartender.
It proves that if you keep on drinking whisky
you will never have worms.

282.

Love.
Life is a sermon;
existence preaches in its own way,
but always indirectly –
and that is the beauty of it.

The harmony in nature teaches,
without any intention,
the lesson of balance in life.
Look at a bird on the wing –
and effortlessly you will go into meditation.
Or listen to its song –
and for no reason your heart will move with it.
And when there is no effort on your part
the meditation goes deep and suddenly transforms you;
and when there is no motivation and you move –
the movement is in the divine.

283.

Love.
I know your inner condition
more than you know it yourself
because now your inner is not my outer.

Things that are happening to you unconsciously
and even against your conscious will *are good*.
Welcome them and be grateful,
because nothing divine can happen to you with your will,
rather, your will is the only barrier.
Say wholeheartedly: *Thy will be done!*
And feel it
and live it.
Come home soon,
I am waiting for you,
and much is waiting to happen to you also.
I know you are skeptical.
That is not bad
but a good beginning to start with.
Wherever there is mind there is skepticism.
Mind is skepticism
and therefore conflict.
That is the way of the mind
and its nature.
Please do not fight with it
nor be identified with it.
These are the obvious alternatives,
but both are false,
and aspects of the same coin.
You will have to walk in between.

Come and be with me, and you will understand.

284.

Dear Mukta.
Love.
Yes, you were related to Yoga Vivek
in one of your past lives.
Now many things will be remembered by you soon
because the key is in your hands.
But do not think about them at all,

otherwise your imagination will get mixed up
with the memories
and then it will be difficult to know
what is real and what is not.
So always be aware from now on
that you do not think about past lives:
let the memories come up by themselves.
No conscious effort on your part is needed;
on the contrary it will be a great hindrance.
Let the unconscious do the work,
you be just a witness,
and as the meditation goes deeper
many locked doors will be opened to you.
But always remember to wait for the mysteries
to reveal themselves.
The seed is broken – and much is to follow.
You need only wait and be a witness.

285.

Love.
Just drop yourself into the divine and be purified!
Surrender and be reborn.
Do not resist.
Let go!

286.

Love.
See: this is a white paper –
it contains words.
You can look at it as white paper or as words.
Or, listen to the silence which contains a sonata;
you can be aware of the silence or of the sonata.
Or, think of the space which contains a building;
you can be aware of the space or of the building.

Or, imagine an empty house;
you can conceive of it as the walls or as an emptiness.

If you see the words, the building,
the sonata and the walls
you are in the mind,
but if you see the white paper or the silence or the space
or the emptiness
then you are in meditation.

287.

Love.
From sound to soundlessness is the path.

Intone a sound like A-U-M,
slowly, and as sound enters soundlessness so do you.

Or: remain in the gap between any two sounds
and you yourself will become soundlessness.
Or: bathe in the continuous sound of a waterfall,
or any other.
Or: by putting your fingers in your ears
hear the source of all sounds –
and there will be a sudden explosion
of the silent music of the cosmos.

Using any way fall into the abyss of soundlessness
and you will achieve the divine.

288.

Love.
I am thrilled with great expectations about you.
Much is to happen within you and without also.
You are on the verge of the explosion,

so be alone.
Not lonely but alone,
and live with that aloneness.
Rather, be that aloneness;
that is the only meditation for you now.
Loneliness is negative:
to be lonely is to be aware of the absence of others.
But to be alone is the most positive state of mind:
it is to be aware of the presence of oneself.

Be aware of the presence that is you.
Just be aware and wait,
wait for the happening.
Near, very near is the moment.
And remember that I am always with you.
I have always been with you
even when you did not know me.

And always feel my blessings.

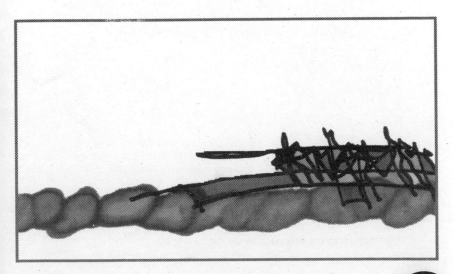

289.

Love.
Takuan says: You cannot bathe in solid ice,
nor can you live in a frozen consciousness –
and what is the mind except that?
Go in and find out.
Do not ask anybody,
do not go to the scriptures,
go in and find out.

Do not think about it
because that is absurd –
how can you think against the mind?
Any conclusion out of thinking
can only strengthen the mind.
Do not think because thinking
is stopping, halting and freezing.
Thinking is the disease.

Go in and find out – *immediately.*
A moment's thinking
and you are again in the old rut.
A moment's thinking
and you are as far from the real as is possible.

290.

Love.
We kneel down to ourselves
because we kneel down to the gods we make
out of our experience, or out of our desires and dreams,
or out of our so-called logic and foolish arguments.
This is neither humility nor prayer,
rather, on the contrary, this is
the most egoistic attitude possible.
The truly religious mind is one which just kneels down –

not to anyone, not to any image in particular.
This kneeling down is nothing but
a flowering of one's total nothingness.
Then this kneeling down becomes an inner way of life,
and unless prayer is such, prayer is not.
One cannot pray, one can only be prayerful.

291.

Love.
You cannot run away from the self
because you are the self –
how can you run away from it?
It is like running from one's own shadow:
all your efforts are bound to be futile.
Rather, stop and see it,
witness it, be aware of it.
Face the shadow and then – where is it?
It has never been, really.
You created it by not facing it
and you strengthened it by running from it.
Is it not time now to stop the game?

292.

Love.
Search – and the ego is always somewhere behind.
Search – and in every act the ego is the motivation.
But if one can find that this is so
and can realize it,
one goes beyond it, because the very realization
is the going beyond.

Brother, said Mulla Nasrudin to a neighbor,
I am collecting to pay the debt of a poor man
who cannot meet his obligations.

Very commendable said the other, and gave him a coin.
Who is this person?
Me, said Nasrudin as he hurried away.

A few weeks later he was at the door again.
I suppose you are calling about a debt,
said the trusting neighbor.
I am.
I suppose someone can't pay a debt
and you want a contribution?
That is so.
I suppose it is you who owes the money?
Not this time.
Well, I am glad to hear it.
Take this contribution,
Nasrudin pocketed the money.
Just one thing, Mulla –
what prompts your humanitarian sentiments
in this particular case?
Well, you see...I am the creditor!

293.

Love.
Knowledge is through experiencing.
Mere information is not knowledge,
on the contrary it cannot give the clarity
which knowledge gives to the mind
and may confuse one more
because a confused mind is still more burdened with it.

Two men had played chess
regularly together for several years.
They were quite evenly matched
and there was keen rivalry between them.
Then one man began to beat his rival
nearly every time they played

and the other man was completely at a loss
to understand this phenomenon.
On the contrary, he was expecting his game to improve
because he was reading a four-volume set
on *How to Play Chess*.
After much thought he came up with an idea.
He sent the books to his friend as a gift –
and it was not long before they were evenly
matched again!

294.

Love.
There is no proof of the divine in the world
for it is hidden deep, deep, deep inside.
But in you there is the absolute proof,
for it is deep, deep, deep, inside.
Go in and discover it.

Thinking about it will not help:
action is needed,
action turned on oneself –
so *act*.
That is, *turn in*.

Man is like a sealed book
written before he was born,
and ordinarily he carries it unopened inside himself
until he dies.
One who opens it knows that *he is not*
and only the divine is.

295.

Love.
Truth is aristocratic.
It cannot be decided by votes or numbers
because truth is enough in itself,
it needs no help or support;
it even needs no proof because truth is self-evident.

A certain man was believed to have died
and was being prepared for burial
when he revived.
He sat up
but he was so shocked at the scene around him
that he fainted.
He was put in a coffin
and the funeral party set off for the cemetery.
Just as they arrived at the grave
he regained consciousness,
lifted the coffin lid
and cried out for help.
It is not possible that he has revived, said the mourners,
because he has been certified as dead
by competent experts.
But I am alive! shouted the man.
He appealed to a well-known and impartial scientist
and jurisprudent who was present.
Just a moment, said the expert.
He then turned to the mourners, counting them:
Now we have heard what
the alleged deceased has had to say;
you fifty witnesses tell me what you regard as the truth.
He is dead, said the witnesses.
Bury him, said the expert.
And so he was buried.

296.

Love.
Choice is the root cause of all anguish.
Choose and you always choose hell —
even when you choose heaven.
And who chooses hell directly?
Yet everyone lives in hell.
What a trick!
The gates of heaven open into hell!

Then what is to be done?
Nothing at all,
because in doing nothing
you can rest content with all things as they are.
and you have knocked at the right door
without even knocking!

297.

Love.
Silence is benediction
but not the silence you can create,
because *you are the noise*
so you cannot create silence.
But you can create the illusion of it,
and this illusion is created by all sorts of
auto-hypnotic techniques.

So never use auto-suggestions to be silent;
rather, be aware of the constantly chattering mind,
and be aware, not to make it still but to understand it.
This very understanding flowers into a silence
which is not just absence of noise
but a positive bliss.

298.

Love.
To explore truth one must be free of one's prejudices –
that is, from oneself.
Otherwise one goes round and round in circles,
because the known can never
be the door for the unknown;
and the known is the mind,
so mind becomes the barrier.
Look attentively at this fact.
Be alert to the vicious circle of the mind –
and then there is transcendence.
The known must cease for the unknown to be.
The known must go for the unknown to come in –
and this cessation of the known is meditation.

299.

Love.
The more deeply you go within yourself
the less you will find yourself –
and yet *that* is the very heart of your being.

And vice versa also:
because the more you go without
the more you will find yourself –
and yet that is the very heart of your non-being.

These are the two ways in which you can go.
The first is the way of meditation,
and the second is the way of the mind.

300.

Love.
Be ordinary, so ordinary that you come to be
virtually nobody –
and there is the opening,
and there is the explosion.
Only when you are not are you the extraordinary!

But do not think about it
and do not crave it,
and if the craving comes – be aware and *laugh*.
It will be stopped by awareness
and the created energy will be used by the laughter,
and after the laugh you will feel a deep relaxation.
Then begin to dance or sing
and the negative state of the mind
will be transformed into the positive.

The craving to be someone, somebody,
is absolutely negative
because the ego is the negation of *being*.

The ego is the principle of negation,
and if the negative is negated then you are positive.
The ego is the source of all inferiority,
but the trick is subtle
because the ego promises superiority
and in the end only results in inferiority.
Decode this secret and understand it very clearly.

One who thinks in terms of superiority
will always remain inferior
because these are two aspects of the same coin.
Sow the seeds of superiority
and you will reap the crop of inferiority.
Begin with the longing for superiority
and you will end up with nothing but inferiority

and all the hell that is involved in it.

Begin with humbleness, with humility,
and you are nearer to the divine.
In fact you are divine
but the ego will not allow you any gap
to look into your own divinity.
On the contrary
it will go on creating new, imaginary heavens
only to make way for new hells.
Enter heaven and you are entering hell!

Beware of this, and beware of your so-called self –
the creator of all the agonies that exist on earth.
Be a *no-self* and you will be that which you are already
and have been always –
that which is bliss eternal,
and freedom,
and the cosmic being, the *brahman*.

Tat twam asi – that art thou, my love.

301.

Love.
Man is unaware of himself.
He does not know what is happening to him,
nor does he know the state of his being.

A man cut down a tree one day.
A Sufi who saw this taking place said:
Look at this fresh branch which is full of sap, and happy
because it does not know yet that it has been cut off.
But his companion said:
Yes, it may be ignorant of the damage it has suffered,
but it will know in due time.
Hearing this the Sufi laughed and said:

Meanwhile you cannot reason with it.

This reverence is the state of man.
this ignorance is the state of man –
and meanwhile you cannot reason with him!
Or can you?

But this is irrelevant.
If you can reason with yourself that is more than enough!

302.

Love.
In life everything is whole, and organically whole.
You cannot divide it
or take it in parts.

Love is like that
and meditation is also like that.
Even death is like that.
That is why I say:
Death is not _dead_ but organically one with life.
You cannot die partially!
 – either you die or you do not die.
Nor can you die gradually.
Please remember this always
when you are in meditation or in prayer or in worship.

A very valuable dachshund
owned by a wealthy woman was run over.
The policeman sent a man
to tell the woman of her misfortune.
But break the news gently, he said.
She thinks a lot of this dog.
The man rapped on the mansion door
and when the woman appeared, he said: Sorry, lady,
but part of your dog has been run over.

303.

Love.
Artificial and outward discipline have no use –
the inner and natural discipline is enough.
But what is the inner discipline?
In one word: *acceptance* –
total acceptance.
And acceptance can be only total
because partial acceptance
is just a contradiction in terms.
If you live – live!
If you die – die!
If you suffer – suffer!
And then there is no problem
and no anxiety
and no anguish –
and what *freedom!*

A Zen master was once asked:
It is terribly hot, how shall we escape it?

Why not go, answered the master,
to the place where it is neither –
neither hot nor cold?

Where is that place?

And then the master laughed and said:
In summer we sweat and in winter we shiver.

304.

Love.
How can a man learn to know himself? enquires Goethe,
and then answers:
Never by reflection but only by action.

John Burroughs doubts this.
He says:
Is not this a half-truth? —
because one can only learn his powers of action by action
and his powers of thought by thinking.

But I say that
man is always more than all his actions and
all his thoughts,
and unless that *more* is known no one knows himself.
That *more* can be known neither
by action nor by reflection
because they both belong to the periphery
and that *more* is eternally the center.
It can only be known through witnessing action
and thought both:
not *by* them but by *witnessing* them.
And witnessing is meditation.

305.

Love.
There is no answer to man's ultimate questions
because the questions are absurd,
and moreover there is no one to answer them.
Existence is silent and has always been so,
so do not ask
but be silent and live it and know it,
because there is no knowing except living.
The search for answers is meaningless.

A patient in a mental hospital
placed his ear to the wall of his room, listening intently.
Quiet! he whispered to an orderly and pointed
to the wall.
The attendant pressed his ear against the wall, listened, and then
said: I don't hear anything.

No, replied the patient.
It's awful, it's always been this way!

306.

Love.
The mind lives in a logical somnambulism,
and it feeds on arguments and words.
You cannot come out of it gradually
or logically or rationally.
Rather, *take the jump*,
illogical and irrational —
and the jump can be nothing else than that.
It cannot be calculated
or conceptualized or predetermined
because it is going into the unknown
and the unchartered
and the unpredictable,
and ultimately not only into the unknown
but into the unknowable also.

307.

Love.
Meditation cannot be taught directly
because it is not a mechanical technique,
but a living art.

Dogo had a disciple called Soshin.
Soshin waited long with his master
to be taught the art of meditation.
He expected lessons the way a schoolboy
is taught at school,
but there no special lessons were forthcoming,
and this bewildered and disappointed the disciple.
One day he said to the master:

It is a long time since I came here
but not a word has been given to me
regarding the essence of meditation.
Dogo laughed at this heartily and said:
What are you saying, my boy?
Since your arrival I have continually
been giving you lessons on the matter!

At this the poor disciple was even more bewildered
and for some time he could not think what to say.

Then one day he gathered courage and asked again:
What kind of lesson could it have been, sir?
Dogo said:
When you bring me a cup of tea in the morning, I take it;
when you serve me a meal, I accept it
and when you bow to me I return it with a nod.
How else do you expect to be taught in meditation?
Soshin hung his head
and began to think about the
puzzling words of the master,
but at this the master said again:
If you want to see, *see, right at once,*
because when you begin to think
you miss the point altogether.

308.

Love.
Meditate, pray and wait.
Do not will anything,
for in you there is strength
greater than any strength of your own.
But it works only when *your will* is at rest.

309.

Love.
Be free at the center;
let the center relax and die:
be only a circumference –
and this is the only renunciation I know.

No man is free until he is free at the center.
When he lets go then he is really free –
and then life is not anguish
and then life is not agony
because no hell can exist without the self, the center.

310.

Love.
Do you hear me?
Do you see me?
I stand at the door and knock,
and I knock because of a promise made
in another life and another age.

311.

Love.
Be in the crowd as if you are alone
and vice versa.
Receive a guest with the same attitude
you have when alone,
and when alone
maintain the same attitude you have in receiving guests.
In this way the drop drops into the ocean.
On retiring, sleep as if you have entered your last sleep,
and upon awakening be reborn again.
In this way the ocean drops into the drop.

312.

Love.
Emptiness is not really emptiness:
rather, it is the all.
It is not negative:
rather, it is positivity itself.
It is out of it that everything is born
and to it everything returns.
It is the source and ground of all existence.
So whenever I say *emptiness*
I never mean just emptiness!
To me emptiness is not the absence of anything

but the presence of *emptiness itself*.
And now you can understand it
because you yourself are in it,
and it is in you.

Once a student asked Joshu: Sir, you teach that
we must empty our minds,
but I have nothing in my mind;
now what shall I do?
The old master laughed and said:
Throw it out!

But I have nothing. How can I throw it out?

If you can't throw it out, carry it out!
Drive it out!
Empty it out!
But don't stand there in front of me with nothing
in your mind!

313.

Love.
Come here whenever it is possible.
You will always be welcomed.
And stay with me a little longer,
and let me help.

It will be difficult for you
because you will have to let go of yourself completely.
But it is not impossible –
and for you especially
because I have seen in you the great potential
that is awaiting its opportunity.

With you much that is impossible is possible.
There is a seed which is longing to explode.

Its very longing is the source of your search,
its longing is the tension that you are today
and its longing will be the freedom
that you will be tomorrow.
The essence is there and
the existence will follow if you so wish.
Please follow its call to the conclusion.

Go on doing meditation.
Do not seek results,
they will come by themselves when the time is ripe.
And the time is ripe
but *you* still are not.

Let meditation ripen you.

314.

Love.
Life is non-fragmentary,
but mind makes it appear fragmentary;
and this fragmentation creates all the problems.
Beware of fragments
and always look beyond them
and below them
and through them –
then you will be able to see the ocean
in spite of all the waves.
The waves are in the ocean
but the waves are not the ocean.
The ocean can be without the waves
but the waves cannot be without the ocean.

315.

Love.
Mind means duality
and meditation, oneness.
In Zen they call it – *The One Sword.*

Kusunoki Masashige came to a Zen monastery
when he was about to meet the oncoming army
of Ashikaga Takanji, and asked the master:
When a man is at the parting of the ways
between life and death, how should he behave?
The master answered: Cut off your dualism
and let *the one sword* stand serenely by itself
against the sky!

316.

Love.
The real thing is
not to fight with your thoughts or desires or instincts
because that is negative
and the negative cannot help.
The real thing is
to grow in awareness, in meditation,
because then one wins without any fight whatsoever.
And to win through conflict is not a real victory
because that which has been suppressed
will have to be suppressed again and again.
Through conflict there is no end to conflict
and through fight only more fight is born.

But there is a victory
without any conflict, fight or suppression.
That victory comes through positive growth in awareness.
Do not fight with yourself
but grow in awareness and understanding and silence,

and all that is negative and diseased
will have withered away by itself.

Suzuki tells a story:
Chi Hsing Tzu was raising a fighting cock for his lord.
Ten days passed and the lord asked:
Is he ready? Chi answered:
No sir, he is not ready.
He is still vain and flushed with rage.

Another ten days passed and the prince asked
about the cock.
Chi said: Not yet, sir.
He is on the alert whenever he sees the shadow
of another cock
or hears its crowing.

Still another ten days passed
and when the inquiry came from the prince, Chi replied:
Not quite yet, sir.
His sense of fighting is still smoldering within him
ready to be awakened.

When another ten days elapsed
Chi replied in response to the inquiry:
He is almost ready.
Even when he hears another crowing he shows
no excitement.
He has now become positive.
He has grown in subtle inner awareness.
Now he resembles one made of wood,
he is so quiet and silent.
His qualities are integrated.
No cock is his match
and to win he will not have to fight
because other cocks will run away from him immediately.
They cannot face him now.

And really it proved so.
He won fights without fighting at all.

And I say that you can do likewise with yourself:
learn the secret from Chi Hsing Tzu's cock!

317.

Love.
Everything has happened as it should happen.
And I was surprised not because you ran away from here
but because I never thought you could be so predictable!
It is not from here that you have escaped,
it is only a vain effort to *escape* from *yourself* –
which is impossible.
How can one escape from oneself?
But in meditation a moment comes,
necessarily comes, when the mind tries the impossible –
for the mind this is the last defensive act.
Meditation is ultimately *suicidal* to the mind.

And of course the mind must be given a chance –
and you have given it!

Meditation is encountering yourself
directly and in your total nakedness.
This creates fear and the futile effort to escape.
The effort is futile because
whatsoever is known once is known forever
and you cannot be the old ignorant person again.
There is no way to go back
and there is no bridge.

This escape will make you more mature too
and you will come back strengthened
through it and because of it.

Now relax there under the sky and beside the sea
and I will be there.
Whenever you are relaxed you will feel my presence.
And when you feel like coming, come back –
and soon you will feel this.
I will be waiting here for you as ever.
Come and continue the arduous journey
towards your self.

318.

Love.
I know that the apprenticeship
is very hard but *worth it*.
So keep on. It is arduous,
but one has to pay for everything,
and in no other way can you get to *the great treasure*.
You have longed for it for lives and lives
and now when the time is ripe
and the key is being given to you
do not lose courage.

Access to the treasure is difficult
because it is hidden
in our own unconscious layers of the mind.
It will be easy if you approach that threshold
when the diurnal tide is favorable,
that is when you are passing from sleep to waking
or from waking to sleep.
So evening and morning
are probably the best times for meditation.
You might have noticed that when the mind
is recovering from sleep it takes at least fifteen minutes
to close one aperture and fully open the other.

That is why dreams
cannot last longer than that

in your memory after waking.
When the mind is approaching sleep
it again passes the same threshold.
Be aware of this threshold
because it is very significant
for those who are in search of the inner treasure.
This threshold is the gate to the unknown.
This threshold,
this gap between waking and sleep,
must be used for meditation.
Be aware of the gap,
be a witness of the interval,
and you will be transformed.

319.

Love.
I know what is happening to you –
nothingness is descending, emptiness is increasing.
Welcome it, and rejoice in its coming.
Dance in ecstasy because
there is no other way to welcome it.
And the more you dance, the more you will die.
And when you are completely dead you will be reborn.
And the moment is near, very near – just by the corner.
You have passed through the entrance-explosion
and now be ready for the ultimate.

Look at yourself once more
as the river looks at itself before falling into the ocean,
because after falling into the ocean
there will be no one to look, and no one to be looked at!

320.

Love.
What is meditation?
Hsu Yun says: Meditation lies in *laying down*.

But laying down what?
Laying down *yourself* – because nothing less will do.

Have you ever been at the bedside of a dead man?
If you try to scold him he will not be excited,
and even if you hit him with a staff he will not hit back.
He also indulged once in the same things everyone indulges in.

He also longed for reputation and wealth.
But now he is without any longing whatsoever.
Now he does not make any distinctions
and lays down *everything*.
If you can be in this laying down state – *alive*,
you are in meditation.

321.

Love.
Leave the grasping of things and thoughts.

Open your fist completely
because grasping is suffering.

Stop! cries Buddha.
But the mad mind does not stop.

If it stops, it is Enlightenment!

322.

Love.
Love to be alone.
Solitude is the temple of the divine,
and remember that there is no other temple.

323.

Love.
Do not be closed to the universe.
Open all your doors and windows
and let everything pass freely in and out, out and in,
because only then will you be able to receive the truth.

324.

Love.
Ego plays a subtle role everywhere –
not only in men but in mice also!

An arrogant elephant
looked down contemptuously at a mouse
and said: You are just about
the skinniest little creature I have ever seen.
I am not always like this, squeaked the mouse.
I've been sick!

325.

Love.
The whole of Yoga has gone dead because of imitation.
One cannot imitate anything that is real.
The real is always spontaneous:
one can jump into it but one cannot practice it.

Any practice is of the mind and by the mind –
and the mind is the past, the dead.
The mind is the thing one has to jump out of.

Out of the mind is the explosion,
so be aware of the mind and its tricks!

Mamiya went to a great teacher to learn meditation.
The teacher told him to concentrate on the famous koan:
What is the sound of one hand?
Mamiya went away
and came back a week later shaking his head.
He could not get it.
Get out! said the master. You are not trying hard enough.
You still think of money and food and pleasure.
It would be better if you died,
then you might learn the answer.

The next week Mamiya came back again.
When the master asked him:
Well, what is the sound of one hand? –
he clutched at his heart, groaned
and fell down as if dead.
Well, you have taken my advice and died,
said the master,
but what about the sound?
Mamiya opened one eye:
I have not solved that yet, he said.
Dead men don't speak, said the master.
Get up and get out!

326.

Love.
We settle down where no settling is possible.
We make homes
whilst homelessness is the very nature

of our consciousness.
We go on doing things which are impossible
and then suffer!
But no one else is responsible.

We fight with the void and are then defeated –
not because the void is stronger than us
but because it is not.

Now stand up
and fight with the empty space of the room
so that you can know and taste
the whole stupidity of the human mind.
And then sit down and laugh at yourself,
and as the laughter dies down
be silent and search within,
and then you will come to know a deep mystery:
the mystery that the void is not only without
but within also!

327.

Love.
Death is everywhere
but everyone deceives himself that it is not for him.
This is the greatest
and the deepest deception the human mind is capable of,
and unless one is constantly aware of this fact
one is bound to be a victim of this deception –
because the mind goes on giving
very beautiful and logical rationalizations
up to the very end.

I have heard about a ninety-year-old man
who got into a bitter argument with his shoemaker
as to how a pair of shoes should be made.
See here, said the shoemaker,

What's the idea of doing so much yapping?
You are past ninety
and there is little chance of your living long enough
to wear these shoes out.
The old fellow looked sternly at the shoemaker
and said: Apparently you are not aware
that statistics prove that very few people
die after ninety years of age!

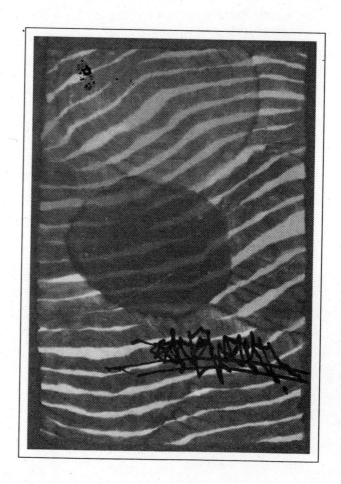

328.

Love.
Information is not knowledge
because information is not transformation
and can never be –
and knowledge comes only through transformation.

Information is adding something to the same old mind.
It is quantitative;
there is no qualitative change
because the mind behind it remains the same.
That is why all that is called education
just proves to be superficial.

Mind must go through a qualitative change,
otherwise there is no wisdom;
and to go on adding information to ignorance is fatal.

I call meditation
the method for mind's total mutation.
First let there be a transformation
of the very quality of the mind
and only then education can be educative.

In ancient times
the king of a certain country was concerned
because his son was something of a fool.
The king's counselors urged that the son be sent away
to a great university in another land
in the hope that the boy
would acquire learning and wisdom.
The king agreed.
The son studied hard for several years
then wrote to his father that he had learned
just about everything possible
and pleaded to be allowed to return home.
The king assented.

When the son arrived at the palace
the king was overjoyed.
A great feast was prepared
and all the great men of the kingdom were invited.
At the end of the festivities
one of the sages present asked the son
what he had learned.
The young man ticked off the university's curriculum
that he had gone through. While the lad was talking
the sage slipped a ring off his finger,
closed his hand over it,
held up his hand and asked: What do I hold in my hand?
The son though for a moment and said;
It is a round object with a hole in the center.
The sage was astonished at such wisdom.
Maybe the lad had become a great mind.
Will you now name the object? asked the sage.
The king's son pondered for a few moments, then said:
The sciences that I studied do not help me
in answering your question,
but my own commonsense tells me that it is a cartwheel.
The sage concluded to himself
that you can educate a fool
but you cannot make him think.

329.

Love.
Yes, there is a *way,*
but in many the will is lacking to find it.
And it is not far away,
it is just by the corner, so to speak.

Knowingly or unknowingly all men long for it.
Really, the whole of life is a longing for it
because without it
there is no reaching, no flowering, no fulfillment.

But few men seek it
and still fewer seek it rightly
and still fewer find it –
and all of those who find it do not enter.
Only a few enter
and still fewer progressively follow it.
But those who follow it with their total being
realize that the way is the goal itself!

330.

Love.
Mind and meditation are two names
of the same substance,
or the same energy.
Mind is energy flowing in dualisms,
in conflict and dis-ease;
and meditation is non-dual energy,
one with itself and at ease.

Thinking is impossible without dualisms,
that is why meditation asks you to go beyond thinking.
The moment there is no thinking –
or a single ripple of thought –
the energy becomes integrated
and there is a qualitative change.
The no-thinking energy
opens the door of the dimensionless dimension.

So refrain from seeking even
Enlightenment or Buddhahood
because with any seeking whatsoever
the mechanism of thought
begins to operate and create dualisms.

331.

Love.
Do not forget the search for the divine
for even a single moment
because the time is always short and the task is great,
and besides, the mind is wavering.
In fact the mind is the wavering.
Remember this, and remain aware of this fact
as much as you can
because the moment one is aware, the wavering stops,
and in the intervals are the glimpses:
glimpses of oneself, glimpses of no-mind.
One has to absolutely transcend the wavering of the mind
before one comes to the doors of the beloved.
No-mindedness is the door.
And the door is not far off.

But the seeker is asleep.
Mind is the sleep.
That is why you will have to be attentive and alert
to everything that passes before your consciousness –
even be attentive to the inattentive moments.

Through constant awareness
the spiritual sleep will be broken
and you will he transformed.
This is your potentiality,
this is everyone's potentiality,
and for you the time is ripe.

But the seed can remain a seed and die.
The opportunity can be lost.
You are free to be that which you are meant to be
or to be that which you are not meant to be.
Man is free to be or not to be –
this is the glory and this is the burden.

Freedom means responsibility,
so be careful.
If you can be that which is your potentiality,
if you can flower in your fullness
then there is bliss
then there is ecstasy, otherwise
ashes are in the hands
and anguish in the heart.
And ultimately everything depends on you:
heaven or hell –
and you and only you will be responsible for it.
So be careful.

My blessings are always with you.

332.

Love.
Metaphysics is born out of childish curiosity,
so however sublime, it remains juvenile.
And all the ultimate answers are foolish in a way
because the ultimate is not only unknown,
it is unknowable.
A mature mind is one
who understands the impossibility
of knowing the ultimate,
and with this understanding
there is a new dimension:
the dimension of *being.*
Knowing is not possible, but *being is.*
Or in other words:
in relation to the ultimate, only *being is knowing.*

This dimension is the religious dimension,
and unless one is religious in this sense
one goes on asking absurd questions
and accumulating even more absurd answers.

In a little backwoods school
the teacher was at the blackboard explaining
arithmetic problems.
She was delighted to see her dullest pupil
paying fixed attention,
which was unusual for him.
Her happy thought was that at last
the lanky lad was beginning to understand.
When she finished she said to him:
You were so interested, Cicero,
that I am sure you want to ask some questions.
Yes'm, drawled Cicero, I got one to ask.
Where do those figures go when you rub them off?

333.

Love.
Do not cling to anything,
to any idea,
because clinging is the bondage.
Even if one is clinging to the idea of liberation –
moksha or nirvana –
one will be in bondage.
With clinging meditation is impossible
because clinging is mind, the bondage;
and no-clinging is meditation –
the freedom.

In the *Book of Amu Daria* there is an old Sufi tale:
Once upon a time there was a monkey
who was very fond of cherries.
One day he saw a delicious looking cherry
and came down from his tree to get it,
but the fruit turned out to be in a clear glass bottle,
so he had to put his hand into the bottle to get it out.
As soon as he had done so
he closed his hand over the cherry

but then he found that he could not
withdraw his fist holding the cherry
because it was larger than the bottle's neck.

Now all this was deliberate
because the cherry in the bottle was a trap laid
by a monkey hunter
who knew how monkeys think.

The hunter, hearing
the monkey's whimperings, came along.
The monkey tried to run away,
but because his hand was, *as he thought,*
stuck in the bottle,
he could not move fast enough to escape.
But *as he thought* he still had hold of the cherry,
he consoled himself.
The hunter picked him up
and tapped the monkey sharply on the elbow
making him suddenly relax his hold on the fruit.
The monkey was now free –
but he was captured.
The hunter had used the cherry and the bottle
and he still had them.

This monkey-way of thinking is the mind-way also!
And in the end when death, the hunter, comes,
everyone is found caught in his own bottle.
Remember, before the hunter comes
make sure your hand is out of the bottle!

334.

Love.
A life without meditation
is like a winter landscape with the sun hidden,
the flowers frozen and the wind whispering

through the withered leaves.

And everyone knows it
because everyone lives it that way,
though no one needs to live it that way.

But why is this so?
This is so because life's needs require an occupied mind
and meditation means being unoccupied.
We train ourselves to be occupied
and then forget that one needs to be unoccupied sometimes
to know the ecstasy of sheer existence.

One is to be totally vacant inside
because only then is one a host to the divine guest.

335.

Love.
Meditation is beyond knowledge.
You can be it but you cannot *know it.*

All knowledge is superficial.
It is never anything else
but an acquaintance from outside.
It is always *about*
but never *the thing itself;*

When the Chinese emperor Wu
came to meet Bodhidharma
he asked the master:
What is the holy, ultimate truth?
Bodhidharma laughed and replied:
Nothing holy, sir,
and it is emptiness itself.
Of course Wu was taken aback, but he asked again:
Then who is the one who at present

stands confronting me?
Bodhidharma simply said:
I don't know.

Do you see the beauty of it?
And the truth?
And the innocence?
And the holiness?·
And the fullness?
And how absolutely ultimate it is?

336.

Love.
It is very easy to progress from one illusion to another
because no foundational transformation is needed.
There is no shaking of the foundations
because you remain the same.

So the real problem is not to change the objects of desire
from the worldly to the other-worldly but to transform oneself;
not to change the seeking but to change the seeker –
otherwise the problem remains as it is,
it just takes new shapes.

But how to change the seeker?
First find out _where it is and what it is,_
and then you will come to know a hidden secret:
the seeker exists only while it is not sought,
and when someone goes out to search for it –
it is never found.
It exists only in ignorance and in darkness;
in awareness it is not.
This realization of _no-self_ is the jump.·

Jump into the unknown.
Jump into the truth.

337.

Love.
Whatever I say is nothing new,
nor is it anything old.
Or it is both –
the oldest and the newest.
And to know it you need not listen to me.

Listen to the birds in the morning
or to the flowers and grass blades in the sun
and you will hear it,
and if you do not know how to listen to them
then you will not know from me either.

So the real thing is not what you listen to
but *how* you listen,
because the message is everywhere, everywhere, everywhere.

Now I will tell you the art of listening:
walk about until exhausted or dance or
do vigorous breathing
and then, dropping to the ground, *listen;*
or repeat your own name loudly until exhausted
and then suddenly stop and *listen;*
or at the point of sleep
when sleep has not yet come
and external wakefulness vanishes,
suddenly be alert and *listen*

And then you will hear me.

338.

Love.
That which is never lost cannot be found,
and to search for it is *absurd.*

But the moment this absurdity is understood
all seeking stops by itself
and that which is never lost is found!
That is why I say:
Seek and you will not find,
because the very seeking is the barrier.
The search itself is the hindrance
because it creates the seeker, the ego,
the illusion that I am.
And I am not.

Do not seek and you will find it:
the *I-am-not-ness.*
This nothingness is the gate.
The Gateless gate.

Riko once asked Nansen
to explain to him the old problem of the goose
in the bottle.
If a man puts a gosling into the bottle, he said,
and feeds the gosling through the bottle's neck
until it grows and grows and becomes a goose —
and then there is simply no more room inside the bottle,
how can the man get it out without killing the goose
or breaking the bottle?

RIKO! shouted Nansen, and gave a great clap
with his hands.
Yes master! said Riko with a start.
See! said Nansen.
The goose is out!

339.

Love.
Meditation requires understanding and not effort,
understanding is essential, not effort,

and remember always that you cannot
substitute understanding with any effort whatsoever.

But what do I mean by understanding?
By understanding I mean – living a natural life.

Of course, you cannot try to be natural,
that is self-contradictory!
You can *be* natural but you cannot try to be natural.
Do you understand this?

Suzuki tells a story:
A monk once asked one of the old Chinese masters:
What is the way?
The master replied: The natural one, the ordinary one,
is the way.
How, continued the monk, am I to be in accord with it?
When you try to be in accord with it, said the master,
then you deviate from it.

Does this mean that one should not try?
No, because that too is a way of trying.
Of course, indirect, but still intentional;
that too will not help.
But just see the dilemma clearly and you are out of it.
Are you not?

340.

Love and blessings.
I received your letter.
I was waiting for it daily since you left.
I know that you have gone far away from here
but I also know that *now* you cannot go away from *me* –
and that nearness is all that counts.

You have come near me in a non-spatial and

non-temporal sense.
The meeting has taken place in the *nowhere*
or in the *everywhere* –
because they mean the same thing.
And the real meeting takes place only in this way.
All else is illusion.

Remember me whenever you need
and you will find me then and there.
Ask anything and *wait* – and you will be answered.

The barriers have fallen from your mind
and you have entered the meditative state.
Now the doors of the divine are open.
Do not hesitate, and take the plunge.
You are completely ready,
just be courageous enough to enter the uncharted
and the unknown.
The call from beyond has come –
now accept the challenge and be fulfilled.

Now close your eyes
and feel me and see me and let my blessings
be showered on you.

341.

Love.
Don't take life so seriously,
because seriousness is a great dis-ease,
and not only a disease but a suicide also.
Be playful – totally,
because that is the only way to be living.
Life is a play, a *leela*, and to know it as such is religion,
and to live it as such is *sannyas* – renunciation.

If you can act and live as if acting and living in a dream

and still be a witness to it
then you will be in the cosmic flow, the *tao*.
And to be in the cosmic flow is to be free –
free from oneself, the ego.
The ego is the seriousness, the disease,
and the *tao*, the egoless existence, is the bliss, the ecstasy.
That is why I have given you such an absurd name!

But I have given it to you knowingly.
I have given it to you so that
you may never be identified with it.
The name is so absurd
that you will have to remain nameless
and a nobody behind it.
The name is such that not only others
but you yourself
will be able to laugh at it.
Swami Krishna Christ!

What a name!
But perfectly suitable in a dream drama,
is it not so?

So feel at ease with it.
and laugh with it, and sing and dance with it,
and be SWAMI KRISHNA CHRIST
with all the letters capitalized!
And always remember that you are nobody.
Always be aware that
you are neither a swami nor a Krishna nor a Christ –
that is what is meant by a swami!
And Krishna himself is not a Krishna,
Christ himself is not a Christ,
because they are nameless, absolutely nameless.
They are nobodies – and that is what makes them divine.
The moment one is identified with any name
one is lost to one's divinity.
Either one can be a name or a reality,

and no one can be both simultaneously.
Really be a name –
and your reality is lost.
Really be a reality –
and your name is just a dream, *maya*.
And what nonsense to be a swami!
But once one is at ease with the no-sense
one transcends it.

Please! Don't try to be sensible
otherwise you will never have any sense at all –
because only stupidity tries to be sensible!
The existence is absurd
and meaningless
and irrational –
and that is why it is so beautiful,
and to be in it, such a blessing!

342.

Love.
Man is free to decide, but not free not to decide –
because not to decide is to decide,
to waver is to decide,
to postpone and evade decision is to decide.
There is no escape:
one must say yes or no.
And there are a thousand ways of saying no,
only one way of saying yes,
and no way of not saying anything at all.
This is the human situation,
and the seeker of truth must be aware of it,
otherwise life is wasted unnecessarily.

A single moment lost cannot be regained –
and we have wasted so many lives –
so decide to decide,

and decide to transform and transcend.
With the decision comes crystallization,
and then one is ready to take the jump into the unknown.

343.

Love.
A traveler stops at an inn:
he passes the night there,
takes his meal,
and as soon as he has done so
he packs and continues his journey again.

As for the host of the inn, he has nowhere to go.

The one who does not stay is the guest,
and the one who stays is the host.
Now who are you –
the guest or the host?

Meditate.
No answer is required,
rather, *realize,*
because all answers belong to the guest
and *realization only* to the host.

But do not believe me, I may be just deceiving you.
Go in and find out for yourself!

344.

Love.
Meditation is the master key.
It can open the doors of the infinite
and it can unlock the mystery of the unknown.
But just by possessing the key nothing is attained.

unless one uses it.

Idries Shah tells a dervish tale:
There was once a wise and very rich man who had a son.
He said to him:
My son, here is a jewelled ring.
Keep it is a sign that you are my successor,
and pass it down on for posterity.
It is of value, of fine appearance,
and it has the added capacity of opening
a certain door to wealth.

Some years later he had another son.
When the son was old enough
the wise man gave him
another ring with the same advice.
The same thing happened in the case of his third
and last son.

When the old man had died and the sons grew up
one after the other claimed primacy for himself
because of his possession of one of the rings.
Nobody could tell for certain which was
the most valuable.
Each son had his adherents,
all claiming a greater value
and more beauty in his own ring.
But the curious thing was that
the door to wealth remained shut
for the possessors of the keys
and even their closest supporters.
They were all too preoccupied with
the problem of precedence,
the possession of the ring, its value and appearance.

Only a few looked for the door to the treasury
of the old man.
The rings had a magical quality too.

Although they were keys
they were not used directly
in opening the door to the treasury.
It was sufficient to look on them
without contention or too much attachment
to one or other of their qualities.

When this had been done
the people who had looked
were able to tell where the treasury was
and could open it merely
by producing the outline of the ring.
The treasuries had another quality too:
they were inexhaustible.

Meanwhile the supporters of the three brothers,
repeated the tales of their ancestors about
the merits of the rings,
each in a slightly different way.
The first community thought they had
already found the treasure
because they had the key.
The second thought that it was allegorical
and so consoled themselves.
And the third transferred the possibility
of opening the door
to a distant and remotely imaginable future
and so for them there was
nothing to do at present.

There is every possibility
for you too to belong to one of these three communities,
because anyone who begins to search
is always prone to fall into the trap of any one
of the three.
Really, these are the three basic tricks the mind can play
to save itself from meditation.
So beware of these old tricks.

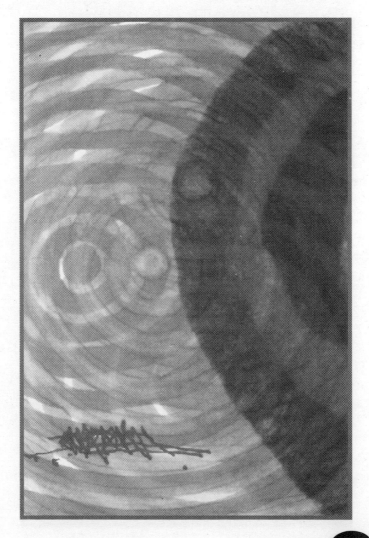

345.

Love.
Look at yourself without thinking, evaluating, or judging,
without any liking or disliking;
that is, without any movement of the mind
or without the noise of the mind.
Then you have eyes
which are altogether different from your eyes
because they are not burdened by the past.
They are innocent and silent,
and in this silence there is neither
the observer nor the observed –
but *that which is*,
undivided and one,
beginningless and endless.

You can call it God or nirvana or anything whatsoever –
the name does not matter
because the name is not the thing,
and when one has known the thing
one does not bother about the value.

346.

Love.
Begin the following meditation from tomorrow –
and know that this is an *order!*
Now you are so totally mine
that I cannot do anything other than order you! Prerequisites:
Do it cheerfully.
Do it relaxedly.
Be playful.
Do it in the morning after taking a bath.

The meditation:
First: breathe deeply and rhythmically,

not fast but slowly,
for ten minutes.
Second: dance rhythmically and slowly;
be ecstatic, as if flowing in it,
for ten minutes.
Third: use the *mahamantra*: hoo-hoo-hoo.
Continue dancing and moving,
do not be serious, do not be tense,
for ten minutes.
Fourth: close the eyes and be silent;
do not move or dance now.
Stand, sit or lie down, as you feel to do,
but just be as if dead,
feel a sinking in,
surrender and be in the hands of the *whole*,
for ten minutes.

Post requirements:
One: live the whole day in ecstasy,
in intoxication of the divine,
flowing and flowering in it,
and whenever depressed say inwardly: hoo-hoo-hoo,
and laugh outwardly,
laugh without any reason, and accept the madness.
Two: before sleep chant the *mahamantra*: hoo-hoo-hoo
for ten minutes,
then laugh at yourself.
Three: in the morning as you feel awake
chant again the *mahamantra*: hoo-hoo-hoo
for ten minutes,

and then begin the day with a hearty laugh.
Four: remember always that I am with you.

347.

Love.
Everything belongs to the man who wants nothing.
Having nothing, he possesses all things in life:
renouncing all he becomes the master of all.
But why?
Because into his emptiness enters the divine.

348.

Love.
Live humbly and in wonder
and then meditation comes by itself.
Relax, and there is ecstasy.
But effort is needed
because unless this fails completely you will not
be effortless!

349.

Love.
Be aware of the mind *before* it is stirred by a thought,
or, be aware of the gap between two thoughts,
and – you will meet yourself!
And this meeting is the meeting with the divine.

350.

Love.
Buddha says: If the mind does not arise
all things are blameless.

What more is there to be said?
And even this much is enough to blame everything!

351.

Love.
The eyes are blind. *One must look within the heart.*
So do not believe the eyes, believe the heart
and remember to look through it,
and then you will come to know things unbelievable.

And unless one comes to know the unbelievable
one has not known at all.

352.

Love.
Remember always the *one* who is inside the body.
Walking, sitting, eating or doing anything,
remember the *one* who is neither walking nor sitting nor eating.

All doing is on the surface,
and beyond all doing is the *being;*
so be aware of the non-doer in the doing.
of the non-mover in the moving.

One day Mulla Nasrudin's wife,
hearing a tremendous thump
ran to his room.
Nothing to worry about, said the Mulla.
It was only my cloak which fell to the ground.
What! And made a noise like that? asked his wife
Yes – I was inside it at the time, said the Mulla.

353.

Love.
A monk asked Daishu Ekai, What is nirvana?
The master answered: Not to commit oneself

to the vicious circle of birth and death
or pleasure and pain
is great nirvana.

What then is the vicious circle
of birth and death and pleasure and pain?

The master said:
To desire nirvana!

Now be silent and feel what is meant by to *desire nirvana*,
and remember that I am not saying *think* about it
because to think is to miss it.
Feel it.
Feel it.
Feel it.

354.

Love.
In this world everything is upside down
and anyone who is meditating
will have to put everything right side up!

One should not try to know life but to know death,
and then the mysteries of life are revealed to him.
One should not ask for any security
and then there is no insecurity at all.

Bunan says in a poem:
While living be a dead man,
be thoroughly dead,
and then behave as you like
because then all is well.

355.

Love.
Materialistic societies produce hollow men,
men with dead emptiness within,
and because of this dead emptiness
one dies before one is really born.

Remember that man cannot live by shops alone,
and today the holy of holies is the shop.

The outer is meaningless without the inner richness,
and the outer richness
only makes the inner poverty prominent.
Man is hollow because there is no inner growth
and the inner grows only when one lives in the inner.

Inward is the way of growth, grace and God.

356.

Love.
Never suppress any thought,
or fight with it,
otherwise you will never be without it.
Fight it, and you invite it more.
Suppress it, and it will be back with double the force.

I have heard
that someone advertised something for women
but with the heading, _Only For Men._
It is reported that
out of ninety thousand women who came across it
eighty-nine thousand nine hundred and ninety-four
read the advertisement.

The other six were blind.

357.

Love.
It is impossible to conceive of the divine intellectually,
and that is why the intellect denies it
or creates fictitious systems about it,
which is even more dangerous than plain denial.
The mind works only in the circle of the known;
it cannot transcend the world of the known.
For the mind the unknown is not.

Says Attar: You know nothing of your real self
here and in this state.
You are like the wax in the honeycomb –
what does it know of fire or guttering?
But when it gets to the stage of the waxen candle
and when light is emitted
then it knows.

358.

Love.
Life is not a detective story,
and you do not have to deduce a thing.
Life is before your eyes as clear as the sun
and as open as the sky.
Just be out of your thinking disease
and open your eyes,
and nothing is hidden at all.
Even the hidden one is not hidden then.

I have heard a dialogue between
Sherlock Holmes and Watson:
Holmes: Ah, Watson, I see you have put on
your winter underwear.
Watson: Marvellous, Holmes, marvellous!
How did you ever deduce that?

Holmes: Well, you have forgotten
to put on your trousers.

359.

Love.
Life goes on flowing.
It does not wait.
But mind thinks and therefore takes time.
To exist, no time is needed,
but to think – time is necessary

Really there is no time in existence.
There appears to be only
because of the mind and its thinking.
Existence exists not in time but in eternity.
It exists in the eternal now.

There is neither past nor future
but only the present –
or not even that –
because without the past and future
it is meaningless to call it present.
Do not live out of the mind,
otherwise you will always lag behind,
because life never waits for you and your so-called mind.
That is why the mind always feels
as if something is missing –
because it is missing life itself – and always!

Once a master said to his disciples:
If you utter a word – thirty blows of my stick for you.
But if you utter no words
just the same, thirty blows of my stick
Now – _speak, speak!_
One disciple came forward
and when he was about to bow

before the master he was struck.
The disciple protested: I have not uttered a single word
nor did you allow me not to utter.
Why the striking ?

The master laughed and said
If I wait for you and your speech or your silence,
it is too late, and life cannot wait!

360.

Love.
Goethe is said to have cried when dying:
Light, light, more light!
And Miguel Unamuno has responded with his:
No – warmth, warmth, more warmth! For we die of cold and not
of darkness!

But I say to you that we die neither because of cold
nor because of darkness
but because of our lust for living
or because of our fear of death –
which is to say the same thing in different ways.

Do not look at death as opposite to life,
because it is not.
And live death moment to moment.
Do not postpone it for the end
because that creates fear. .
Die each moment to the past,
and then each moment you will be fresh,
young and reborn.
And then there is always light
because the very darkness becomes light;
and warmth also,
because only the dead past is cold.
The present is always warm.

361.

Love.
Man is not the end
but only the means.
Man is not really a being
but only a tension
between two planes of being.
Man is only a bridge,
that is why he cannot remain satisfied with himself.
His heart is nothing but a continent of discontent
and his very being is anguish.

Religion is man's wish to pass beyond himself
as he now is.
That is why I say man can never be irreligious;
that is impossible.
He can pretend to be but he cannot be.
Religion is not something accidental or circumstantial,
it is in the very nature of man:
man is a religious animal.
And man is nothing if he is not a desire
to transcend himself.
He can go below himself,
or he can go above,
but he cannot remain himself.
He cannot be at rest.
That is why there is restlessness.

362.

Love.
Use dreaming consciously as meditation
and know well that conscious dreaming opens
new doors of perception.
Lie down, relax,
and dream, but do not fall asleep;

remain conscious in the background.
Wait and watch;
dream anything that happens to your mind.
Do not plan beforehand –
dream anything, because in dream
the whole world is yours.
Dream your existence as you please;
dream and be content...
content with your dreams because they are yours.
And remember that nothing can be yours
like your dreams are
because you yourself are a dream entity! –
and also because your wishes
come to be true in your dreams,
and only in your dreams.

But do not fall into identification.
Be a witness.
Remain aware.
And then suddenly there will be no dreaming.
Only you
and illumination.

363.

Love.
You write to me that
without me you cannot pass through the gate
and with me you will not pass through the gate.
I know that!
But you need not do either.
You need not pass through the gate
with me or not with me,
because I am *the gate*.
I am *no-one*, so how can you be with me or not with me?
And only one who is no one can be the gate.
The gate means the emptiness

because the gate is nothing
but the space to pass through.
Pass through me –
not with me –
and know.
I appear to be someone only from without,
but the deeper you penetrate me
the less you will find me.
And in the end – *no one.*

364.

Love.
Walk as if you are not walking,
stand as if you are not standing,
sit as if you are not sitting –
and then you will begin to feel
something completely new arising within you.
This is the *real* one.
The false you walks, stands and sits,
and the real you just remains in *suchness.*
Fee this – *this very moment,*
because there is no need to postpone it.
And if you postpone it you postpone it forever
because there is no tomorrow for *the real one,*
there is no *there* for it,
it is always *here and now.*

365.

Love.
You will become more deeply tied
to whatever you desire to become free from.
Because freedom is not negation.
Freedom is not 'from something' or 'for something'.
Freedom is not positive either.

Freedom is the transcendence
of negation and affirmation both.
Freedom means freedom from duality.
Where is a 'for or against' there?
With what to react?
What rebellion?
Reaction is not wisdom.
And, rebellion is nothing but a continuity of the old.
Hence, understand – do not fight.
When has anybody attained anything through fighting?
Except pain? – except defeat?
Hence, do not escape, but wake up.
By escaping one has to keep on escaping.
And then there is no end to that.
Knowing is freedom.
Not the fear, not the anger,
not the enmity, not the rebellion.
Only knowing is freedom.

AN INVITATION TO EXPERIENCE

OSHO
**Never Born
Never Died
Only Visited This
Planet Earth Between
Dec 11, 1931 - Jan 19, 1990**

Osho is an enlightened Mystic.

During the course of thirty years of talks to seekers and friends, Osho would answer their questions, or comment on the teachings of the world's great sages and scriptures. His talks continue to bring fresh insight to everything, from the obscure Upanishads to the familiar sayings of Gurdjieff, from Ashtavakra to Zarathustra. Osho speaks with equal authority on the Hassids and the Sufis, the Bauls, Yoga, Tantra, Tao and Gautama the Buddha. And ultimately, Osho concentrates on transmitting the unique wisdom of Zen, because, He says, Zen is the one spiritual tradition whose approach to the inner life of human beings has weathered the test of time and is still relevant to contemporary humanity. Zen is another word for the original Hindi word Dhyana. In English you may translate it as 'meditation', but Osho says this is a poor translation. So call it Dhyana or Zen or whatever you may wish - Osho's emphasis is on *experiencing*.

Osho settled in Pune in 1974, and disciples and friends from all over the world gathered around Him to hear His talks and practice His meditation techniques for the modern man. Western therapeutic group processes, classes and trainings were gradually introduced so bridging the wisdom and understanding of the East with the scientific approach of the West. And now Osho Commune International has evolved into the world's largest centre for meditation and spiritual growth, and offers hundreds of different methods for exploring and experiencing the inner world.

Every year, thousands of seekers from all over the world come to celebrate and meditate together in Osho's buddhafield. The commune grounds are full of lush green gardens, pools and waterfalls, elegant snow-white swans and colourful peacocks, as well as beautiful buildings and pyramids. Such a peaceful and harmonious atmosphere makes it very easy to experience the inner silence in a joyful way.

For detailed information to participate in this Buddhafield contact:

OSHO COMMUNE INTERNATIONAL
17, KOREGAON PARK, PUNE-411001, MS, INDIA
PH: 020 628562 FAX: 020 624181
E-MAIL: commune@osho.net
INTERNET WEB SITE: http://www.osho.com

BOOKS BY OSHO

english language editions

EARLY DISCOURSES AND WRITINGS
A Cup of Tea
Dimensions Beyond The Known
From Sex to Superconsciousness
The Great Challenge
Hidden Mysteries
I Am The Gate
Psychology of the Esoteric
Seeds of Wisdom

MEDITATION
And Now and Here (Vol 1 & 2)
In Search of the Miraculous (Vol 1&.2)
Meditation: The Art of Ecstasy
Meditation: The First and Last Freedom
Vigyan Bhairav Tantra
(boxed 2-volume set with 112 meditation cards)
Yaa-Hoo! The Mystic Rose

BUDDHA AND BUDDHIST MASTERS
The Dhammapada (Vol 1-12)
   The Way of the Buddha
The Diamond Sutra
The Discipline of Transcendence (Vol 1-4)
The Heart Sutra The Book of Wisdom
   (combined edition of Vol 1 & 2)

BAUL MYSTICS
The Beloved (Vol 1 & 2)

KABIR
The Divine Melody
Ecstasy: The Forgotten Language
The Fish in the Sea is Not Thirsty
The Great Secret
The Guest
The Path of Love
The Revolution

JESUS AND CHRISTIAN MYSTICS
Come Follow to You (Vol 1-4)
I Say Unto You (Vol 1 & 2)
The Mustard Seed
Theologia Mystica

JEWISH MYSTICS
The Art of Dying
The True Sage

WESTERN MYSTICS
Guida Spirituale   *On the Desiderata*
The Hidden Harmony
   The Fragments of Heraclitus
The Messiah (Vol 1 & 2)   *Commentaries on*
   Khalil Gibran's The Prophet
The New Alchemy: To Turn You On
   Commentaries on Mabel Collins'
   Light on the Path
Philosophia Perennis (Vol 1 & 2)
   The Golden Verses of Pythagoras
Zarathustra: A God That Can Dance
Zarathustra: The Laughing Prophet
   Commentaries on Nietzsche's
   Thus Spake Zarathustra

SUFISM
Just Like That
Journey to the Heart (same as Until You Die)
The Perfect Master (Vol 1 & 2)
The Secret
Sufis: The People of the Path (Vol 1 & 2)
Unio Mystica (Vol 1 & 2)
The Wisdom of the Sands (Vol 1 & 2)

TANTRA
Tantra: The Supreme Understanding
The Tantra Experience
   The Royal Song of Saraha
   (*same as* Tantra Vision, Vol 1)
The Tantric Transformation
   The Royal Song of Saraha
   (*same as* Tantra Vision, Vol 2)

THE UPANISHADS
Heartbeat of the Absolute
   Ishavasya Upanishad
I Am That *Isa Upanishad*
Philosophia Ultima *Mandukya Upanishad*
The Supreme Doctrine   *Kenopanishad*
Finger Pointing to the Moon
   Adhyatma Upanishad
That Art Thou *Sarvasar Upanishad,*
   KaivalyaUpanishad, Adhyatma Upanishad
The Ultimate Alchemy
   Atma Pooja Upanishad (Vol 1& 2)
Vedanta: Seven Steps to Samadhi
   Akshaya Upanishad

TAO

The Empty Boat
The Secret of Secrets
Tao: The Golden Gate
Tao: The Pathless Path
Tao: The Three Treasures
When the Shoe Fits

YOGA

Yoga: The Alpha and the Omega (Vol 1-10)

ZEN AND ZEN MASTERS

Ah, This!
Ancient Music in the Pines
And the Flowers Showered
A Bird on the Wing
   (same as Roots and Wings)
Bodhidharma: The Greatest Zen Master
Communism and Zen Fire, Zen Wind
Dang Dang Doko Dang
The First Principle
God is Dead: Now Zen is the Only
   Living Truth
The Grass Grows By Itself
The Great Zen Master Ta Hui
Hsin Hsin Ming: The Book of Nothing
   Discourses on the Faith-Mind of Sosan
I Celebrate Myself: God is No Where,
   Life is Now Here
Kyozan: A True Man of Zen
Nirvana: The Last Nightmare
No Mind: The Flowers of Eternity
No Water, No Moon
One Seed Makes the Whole Earth Green
Returning to the Source
The Search: Talks on the 10 Bulls of Zen
A Sudden Clash of Thunder
The Sun Rises in the Evening
Take it Easy (Vol 1) Poems of Ikkyu
Take it Easy (Vol 2)Poems of Ikkyu
This Very Body the Buddha   Hakuin's Song
   of Meditation
Walking in Zen, Sitting in Zen
The White Lotus
Yakusan: Straight to the Point of
   Enlightenment
Zen Manifesto : Freedom From Oneself
Zen: The Mystery and the Poetry of the
   Beyond
Zen: The Path of Paradox (Vol 1, 2 & 3)
Zen: The Special Transmission

ZEN BOXED SETS

The World of Zen (5 volumes)
Live Zen
This. This. A Thousand Times This
Zen: The Diamond Thunderbolt
Zen: The Quantum Leap from Mind to
   No-Mind
Zen: The Solitary Bird, Cuckoo of the Forest

Zen: All The Colors Of The Rainbow (5 vol.)
The Buddha: The Emptiness of the Heart
The Language of Existence
The Miracle
The Original Man
Turning In
Osho: On the Ancient Masters of Zen (7 vol.)
Dogen: The Zen Master
Hyakujo: The Everest of Zen – With Basho's
   haikus
Isan: No Footprints in the Blue Sky
Joshu: The Lion's Roar
Ma Tzu: The Empty Mirror
Nansen: The Point Of Departure
Rinzai: Master of the Irrational
Each volume is also available individually.

RESPONSES TO QUESTIONS

Be Still and Know
Come, Come, Yet Again Come
The Goose is Out
The Great Pilgrimage: From Here to Here
The Invitation
My Way:The Way of the White Clouds
Nowhere to Go But In
The Razor's Edge
Walk Without Feet, Fly Without Wings
   and Think Without Mind
The Wild Geese and the Water
Zen: Zest, Zip, Zap and Zing

TALKS IN AMERICA

From Bondage To Freedom
From Darkness to Light
From Death To Deathlessness
From the False to the Truth
From Unconsciousness to Consciousness
The Rajneesh Bible (Vol 2-4)
The Rajneesh Upanishad

THE WORLD TOUR

Beyond Enlightenment   Talks in Bombay
Beyond Psychology   Talks in Uruguay
Light on the Path   Talks in the Himalayas
The Path of the Mystic   Talks in Uruguay
Sermons in Stones   Talks in Bombay
Socrates Poisoned Again After 25 Centuries
   Talks in Greece
The Sword and the Lotus   Talks in the
   Himalayas
The Transmission of the Lamp   Talks in Uruguay

OSHO'S VISION FOR THE WORLD

The Golden Future
The Hidden Splendor
The New Dawn
The Rebel
The Rebellious Spirit

THE MANTRA SERIES
Hari Om Tat Sat
Om Mani Padme Hum
Om Shantih Shantih Shantih
Sat-Chit-Anand
Satyam-Shivam-Sundram

PERSONAL GLIMPSES
Books I Have Loved
Glimpses of a Golden Childhood
Notes of a Madman

INTERVIEWS WITH THE WORLD PRESS
The Last Testament (Vol 1)

INTIMATE TALKS BETWEEN MASTER AND DISCIPLE – DARSHAN DIARIES
A Rose is a Rose is a Rose
Be Realistic: Plan for a Miracle
Believing the Impossible Before Breakfast
Beloved of My Heart
Blessed are the Ignorant
Dance Your Way to God
Don't Just Do Something, Sit There
Far Beyond the Stars
For Madmen Only
The Further Shore
Get Out of Your Own Way
God's Got A Thing about You
God is Not for Sale
The Great Nothing
Hallelujah!
Let Go!
The 99 Names of Nothingness
No Book, No Buddha, No Teaching, No Disciple
Nothing to Lose but Your Head
Only Losers Can Win in This Game
Open Door
Open Secret
The Shadow of the Whip
The Sound of One Hand Clapping
The Sun Behind the Sun Behind the Sun
The Tongue-Tip Taste of Tao
This Is It
Turn On, Tune In and Drop the Lot
What Is, Is, What Ain't, Ain't

Won't You Join The Dance?

COMPILATIONS
Bhagwan Shree Rajneesh: On Basic Human Rights
Jesus Crucified Again, This Time in Ronald Reagan's America
Priests and Politicians: The Mafia of the Soul

GIFT BOOKS OF OSHO QUOTATIONS
A Must for Contemplation Before Sleep
A Must for Morning Contemplation
Gold Nuggets
More Gold Nuggets
Words From a Man of No Words
At the Feet of the Master

PHOTOBOOKS
Shree Rajneesh: A Man of Many Climates, Seasons and Rainbows *through the eye of the camera*
Impressions... *Osho Commune International Photobook*

BOOKS ABOUT OSHO
Bhagwan: The Buddha for the Future
by Juliet Forman, S.R.N., S.C.M., R.M.N.
Bhagwan Shree Rajneesh: The Most Dangerous Man Since Jesus Christ
by Sue Appleton, LL.B., M.A.B.A.
Bhagwan: The Most Godless Yet the Most Godly Man *by Dr. George Meredith, M.D. M.B.B.S. M.R.C.P.*
Bhagwan: One Man Against the Whole Ugly Past of Humanity *by Juliet Forman, S.R.N., S.C.M., R.M.N.*
Bhagwan: Twelve Days That Shook the World
by Juliet Forman, S.R.N., S.C.M., R.M.N.
Was Bhagwan Shree Rajneesh Poisoned by Ronald Reagan's America?
by Sue Appleton, LL.B. M.A.B.A.
Diamond Days With Osho
by Ma Prem Shunyo

GIFTS
Zorba the Buddha Cookbook

For Osho Books & Audio/Video Tapes Contact :

SADHANA FOUNDATION
17, KOREGAON PARK, PUNE-411001, MS, INDIA
PH: 020 628562, FAX: 020 624181
E-MAIL: distrib@osho.net
INTERNET WEBSITE: http://www.osho.com

DIAMOND POCKET BOOKS
Presents in OSHO BOOKS
Osho's illuminating and
enlightening discourses

BOOK REVIEW

**[The Mystery Beyond Mind;
The Centre of the Cyclone; Be Oceanic;
Love and Meditation;
Meditation the Ultimate Adventure]**

These five above mentioned books are the transcribed version of the lectures given by Osho in Bombay about five years back. These books or the 'Upnishads' as the author himself brands them, are in the question-answer form. Questioned by his disciples on the various physical, physiological and para-psychological aspects of human life vis-a-vis nature, the master seer explains them in a most lucid yet somewhat laconic manner, punctuating his observations with very cogent and witty ancedotes. Delving deep into the phenomenon of the astral and physical world, the author takes the reader beyond the perview of mind and questions the very purpose of human existence and its utility in the universe. Explaining the most abstract meta-physical conceptions by his erudite scholarship Osho admirably succeeds in shedding off the slough of obscurantist learning to bring out the pristine reality. What makes these books of this set eminently readable is the way of their presentation. The well-syntaxed small sentences leave no scope for any ambiguity whatever. This master orator has the knack of elucidating the most ephemeral and abstract concept by most modern scientific terms. In his book 'The Centre of the Cyclone' how deftly he uses the phenomenon of a cyclone to explain the enveloping thoughts that keep the mind at rest like the eye of the cyclone. Osho is the most modern thinker of our times whose arguments rest on the solid scientific reasoning.

 (Price Rs. 30.00 each)

DIAMOND POCKET BOOKS

X-30, Okhla Industrial Area, Phase-II, New Delhi-110020
Ph. : 011-6822803; 6822804; Fax 91-011-6925020

*RECEIVE BOOKS AT HOME BY V.P.P. POSTAGE Rs. 10/- (Extra)
ON ORDER OF THREE OR MORE BOOKS POSTAGE FREE*

BOOK REVIEW

[A Song Without Words; Inner Harmony ; Sing, Dance, Rejoice; Secret of Disciplehood]

One may agree or disagree with what Osho say in these books which are the transcribed version of the thoughts he expressed before a live audience almost spontaneously when questioned by the audience comprising most of his disciples, but one just can't ignore his views. These are the views very powerfully expressed by a mind imbued with great learning yet retaining its originality. Lambasting at the practices performed as the sacred rituals both in the East and the West, and exploding the myth of the belief held sacrosanct by its adherents, Osho brings a fresh breeze of original thinking to understand which the reader of his books needs no special dictionary or terminological expertise considered so necessary to decipher the meaning of other great 'thinkers'. The beauty of these thought provoking books is that you feel as though the author is talking only to you, sitting across the table. As if controlling the reader's thought process he has a knack of quelling the doubts almost automatically, which do surface in the mind of the reader of his books. These neatly printed set of books is as engripping as a crime-thriller or a cliff-hanging suspense book. It is difficult to lay any of these books down once you have started to read them. Sometimes his thoughts resound as echo in your mind and one does feel the pleasure of this unique unison. Discussing physical, social, spiritual problems with equal ease, Osho stands head and shoulders above all the modern thinkers of our time.

(Price Rs. 30.00 each)

DIAMOND POCKET BOOKS

X-30, Okhla Industrial Area, Phase-II, New Delhi-110020
Ph. : 011-6822803; 6822804; Fax 91-011-6925020

RECEIVE BOOKS AT HOME BY V.P.P. POSTAGE Rs. 10/- (Extra)
ON ORDER OF THREE OR MORE BOOKS POSTAGE FREE